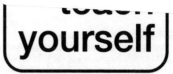

how to win at
online gambling
belinda levez

For over 60 years, more than
40 million people have learnt over
750 subjects the **teach yourself**
way, with impressive results.

be where you want to be
with **teach yourself**

For UK order enquiries: please contact Bookpoint Ltd, 130 Milton Park, Abingdon, Oxon OX14 4SB. Telephone: +44 (0) 1235 827720. Fax: +44 (0) 1235 400454. Lines are open 09.00–18.00, Monday to Saturday, with a 24-hour message answering service. Details about our titles and how to order are available at www.teachyourself.co.uk

For USA order enquiries: please contact McGraw-Hill Customer Services, PO Box 545, Blacklick, OH 43004-0545, USA. Telephone: 1-800-722-4726. Fax: 1-614-755-5645.

For Canada order enquiries: please contact McGraw-Hill Ryerson Ltd, 300 Water St, Whitby, Ontario L1N 9B6, Canada. Telephone: 905 430 5000. Fax: 905 430 5020.

Long renowned as the authoritative source for self-guided learning – with more than 40 million copies sold worldwide – the **teach yourself** series includes over 300 titles in the fields of languages, crafts, hobbies, business, computing and education.

British Library Cataloguing in Publication Data: a catalogue record for this title is available from the British Library.

Library of Congress Catalog Card Number: on file.

First published in UK 2006 by Hodder Education, 338 Euston Road, London, NW1 3BH.

First published in US 2006 by Contemporary Books, a Division of the McGraw-Hill Companies, 1 Prudential Plaza, 130 East Randolph Street, Chicago, IL 60601 USA.

This edition published 2006.

The **teach yourself** name is a registered trade mark of Hodder Headline.

Typeset by Transet Limited, Coventry, England.
Printed in Great Britain for Hodder Arnold, a division of Hodder Headline, 338 Euston Road, London, NW1 3BH, by Cox & Wyman Ltd, Reading, Berkshire.

Hodder Headline's policy is to use papers that are natural, renewable and recyclable products and made from wood grown in sustainable forests. The logging and manufacturing processes are expected to conform to the environmental regulations of the country of origin.

Impression number   10 9 8 7 6 5 4 3 2 1
Year   2010 2009 2008 2007 2006

contents

introduction

Many people gamble online with varying degrees of success. Some win money but a lot lose. Many of these losses could be avoided. They are often due to a lack of knowledge about the games and poor methods of play. Too many people rely on luck instead of skill.

Some games are simply not worth playing because they give poor returns to the player. Others that give a fairer chance may incorporate some bets that are not worth bothering with.

This book aims to teach you how profitable the various games are so that you can make an informed choice about those that are worth playing. The rules are also described so that you can learn how to play properly. You will be taught how to get better value for money, as well as the methods of play that maximize winnings while keeping losses to a minimum. Many illustrated example are given to make the understanding of the games easier.

The issues that you need to consider when gambling are covered, along with advice on where to gamble. The dangers involved with playing with unregulated sites are highlighted and you are also shown how to play safely on the internet to avoid the many online gambling scams.

By the end of the book you should be a more informed gambler with a better understanding of the subject. With plenty of practice, you should also become a more skilful player and, it is to be hoped, a winner instead of a loser.

Good luck!

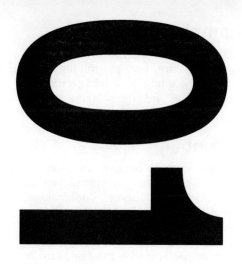

01

internet gambling

In this chapter you will learn:
- about types of online gambling
- the history of online gambling
- about the law
- how to get started with online gambling.

What is online gambling?

Online gambling, also referred to as internet gambling, is placing bets via a computer connection over the internet. You can bet on all forms of gambling including horse and greyhound racing, sports, casino games, lotteries and sweepstakes.

Types of online gambling

There are a number of different ways to bet over the internet, including via bookmakers, betting exchanges, spread betting firms, online casinos and online card rooms. Bookmakers, betting exchanges and spread betting firms take bets on horse racing and sporting events such as football, cricket and golf. Bookmakers provide bets at fixed odds. Betting exchanges allow customers to decide their own prices. Spread betting firms make predictions about events and the customers decide how correct the predictions are. Online casinos give players the opportunity to play games that are traditionally offered in bricks and mortar casinos. This includes roulette, blackjack, dice, punto banco, poker and slots. Online card rooms provide the facilities for playing poker against other players from around the world.

The history of online gambling

Online gambling has seen huge growth since the first online casino, operated by Internet Casinos Inc. (ICI), opened on 18 August 1995. By 1997 the number of online casinos had grown to 30. In 2003 there were over 44,000 online gambling sites. An estimated 12 million people were gambling online, with approximately 3 million from Great Britain (spending £3.5 billion), 4.5 million from the United States and 4 million from Asia. The number of online gambling sites continues to grow, with an estimated 53,000 by 2004.

Is online gambling legal?

Depending on where you live, online gambling may or may not be legal. In many countries legislation has yet to catch up with the phenomenon of internet gambling. Much gambling legislation is outdated. As the legal situation may change at any time, you are advised to check the legality of online gambling in your jurisdiction before placing any bets.

In the UK, the Gambling Act 2005 legislates remote betting. Remote betting includes all types of betting where the parties involved in a bet are not face to face. This includes betting over the internet, telephone, via your television and any future technology that may come into being. The Gambling Act 2005 replaces most of the existing law about gambling in Great Britain. A new organization known as the Gambling Commission was formally established on 1st October 2005 and is responsible for controlling gambling by regulating and licensing operators. Licensed gaming sites on the internet will carry a kitemark to show that the necessary standards have been met.

Betting exchanges come under the category of betting intermediaries and are required to have a betting intermediary operating licence from the Gambling Commission. They are required to keep customers' money in ringfenced accounts.

Spread betting is classified in a different way. Due to its connection to trading on financial markets, all UK spread betting firms are regulated by the Financial Services Authority (FSA), an independent watchdog set up by government under the Financial Services and Markets Act 2000 to regulate financial services in the UK. The FSA has a firm check service, where you can find out if a firm is regulated and who to contact in the firm if you have an enquiry or complaint.

The FSA gives spread betting customers a certain degree of protection. If you have a complaint that you think has not been satisfactorily dealt with by the firm, you have access to the Financial Ombudsman Scheme. In addition, if a spread betting firm goes bust, you have access to the Financial Services Compensation Scheme. The FSA website gives details about how to complain (see taking it further, page 193).

In Australia, the Interactive Gambling Act 2001 prohibits online casino gambling but allows interactive sports betting and wagering services.

In the United States, online horse racing betting for operators authorized by American states is allowed. With online casino gambling the situation is less clear. The Wire Act is often cited as the appropriate legislation covering internet betting but this deals specifically with operating a *sports* betting business. Case law appears to show that online gambling is legal but the US Justice Department insists otherwise. In November 2004 Antigua and Barbuda won a World Trade Organization ruling that United States legislation criminalizing internet betting violates global laws.

How does internet gambling compare with offline gambling?

With internet gambling you are not restricted by local opening hours of casinos and betting shops. You can bet 24 hours a day, seven days a week in the privacy of your own home. With poker, for example, you will always find a game on. Games can be played for money or simply for amusement.

Betting over the internet does have its financial advantages. The costs of operating online gambling firms are considerably cheaper than those of offline firms. These savings are often passed on to the customer in the form of low commission charges and bonuses. For example, betting exchanges charge commission of just 5 per cent or less, with loyal customers often being charged lower rates. As a comparison, a traditional bookmaker will charge around 17 to 20 per cent. With horse racing and sports betting prices can be up to 20 per cent better than with traditional bookmakers. There are also savings to be made with online casinos. With bricks and mortar casinos, you may have to pay admission costs, membership fees and travelling costs. There are none of these costs with online casinos. Many internet betting firms are located offshore. This means that bets are often tax free although this may change later with any new legislation. Players do, of course, have to bear some costs. You will need to invest in a computer and subscribe to the internet.

In casino games, software is used to make the games random. For example, with roulette there is no dealer spinning the ball, instead a random number generator selects the winning number. With card games computer software with a random number generator determines the order of the cards dealt. Games are played at a much faster pace. This is because the human factor is removed and computers are used to deal cards, place bets and calculate payouts.

Social contact is limited. With online poker, for example, you don't see your opponents. This means that you cannot assess someone's likely hand through body language as you would in a traditional game. You can, however, chat to them via the site's messaging service.

Getting started with online gambling

You will need a computer with an internet connection. Ideally, you should have a high-speed connection to keep as up to date as possible with rapidly changing prices and to ensure that your bets are speedily communicated to the betting firm's server. If you play casino games, there will often be a time limit placed on the amount of time in which you have to make a decision.

You will also need an account with an online gambling firm. To get an account you will need to register and deposit money. The general requirements are that you are over 18 years of age and live in a place where internet betting is legal. Proof of your age and residence may be required. You will need to ensure that you comply with your own local, national or state laws before opening an account or placing a bet.

The websites of major gambling sites are given at the end of the book (see taking it further, page 193). Before signing up with a firm you should thoroughly check them out to ensure that they are fair and ethical (see page 11).

Registration involves selecting a user name and password that you will need to log on to the site. You should keep your password secret to stop other people logging on to your account and placing bets. You will also need an email address so that you can be contacted by the internet company.

Depositing and withdrawing money

Some firms require you to deposit money with them before you can start betting, others offer credit facilities. Accounts are often available in a choice of currencies. Money can be deposited in various ways including credit cards, debit cards, cheques, money orders etc. For speed, credit cards and debit cards are ideal. They allow you to directly deposit funds and start betting immediately.

Downloading and installing software

Before you start playing, you will need to download and then install software onto your computer. The software will run the game programs. A site will list the minimum system requirements needed to play their software.

A site will typically show:

- the version of Windows that is supported
- download size – how much space you need on your hard disk to install the software and how quickly this will download
- amount of RAM required
- minimum requirements for your modem.

The software will connect you with the gambling site and allow you to bet or play the games. It will keep a history of bets made or games played. For example, with online poker, the software keeps records of the hands that have been played. This gives you the opportunity to analyse and make improvements to your game.

Playing casino games

To start playing you will need to log on to your account at the casino website. You will then enter the 'lobby' where you will be given a choice of games. A game is selected by moving your mouse pointer to the name of the game and clicking. You will then be taken to a screen that shows the betting layout and the number of chips or amount of money that you wish to spend. To start playing, you need to make an initial bet. The way that bets are placed may vary. Often bets are made by clicking on and dragging the chips to the appropriate place on the betting layout. Alternatively, you may be prompted to key in a betting amount. You will be given instructions about what to do next. For example, with blackjack and other card games there will be a 'deal button' to click on, with dice there is a 'roll button' and roulette will have a 'spin button'. Payouts will be calculated automatically and added to your balance.

02

playing safe

In this chapter you will learn:
- safety aspects of online gambling
- common scams
- how to protect yourself.

How safe is online gambling?

Although internet betting offers greater convenience to the customer it does need to be treated with some caution. The internet is a highly competitive business environment and many businesses have been trading for a relatively short time. A number of sites have gone bust owing customers money. Betting on the internet is a relatively new phenomenon and there is a lack of control and legal framework to deal with some problems that may arise. There are also a number of scam sites that have failed to pay out to customers. Be extremely cautious of betting with unregulated sites in foreign jurisdictions. If a site goes bust, it will be virtually impossible for you to get your money back.

UK companies

UK betting exchange operators are expected to abide by the code of practice for betting exchanges. This provides a framework for a safe and fair betting environment.

It includes the following provisions:

- that the funds of betting exchange customers be ringfenced from the operator's funds so that they are segregated at all times
- there must always be a reserve fund to clear all accounts at any time
- they must adhere to the betting dispute resolution decisions of an external arbitrator, e.g. IBAS (Independent Betting Arbitration Service).

There are safeguards to allow you to control the amount that you bet. This includes daily/weekly deposit limits that you can decide in advance. They also have self-exclusion schemes that allow you to opt out on request allowing you to have your account closed for six months.

Common scams

Fraudulent sites

It is extremely easy to set up a fraudulent site. These sites will typically copy the page designs of established legitimate sites. They will contain the logos of legitimate companies showing that their software has been audited or that they are a member of a trade association. They may show excellent reviews from respected sources. However, if you deposit money with the site, you will receive no payout. The site may be on the internet for only a short time before it is closed down, but if it appears to be a legitimate company a lot of people can be conned in that time. Don't forget – casinos can write their own reviews and post them all over the internet. Some casinos have even been known to set up fake watchdog organizations and to write themselves excellent reviews.

Payment problems

Failure to pay is common. A site appears to be legitimate, so you deposit money with it and start playing. You then cash out but no money is sent to you. A site that fails to pay may then start bombarding you with mail in the name of a different company. They already know that you are a gambler and will try to induce you into depositing money with offers of huge bonuses. There are some sites that pay out but only after a very long time. They hold on to your money, thereby earning themselves interest.

Prize scams

The internet is rife with prize and lottery scams. For example, you may be contacted and told that you have won £1 million in a lottery and that the money is being held for you. You will be given some reason why you have to pay, for example, £100 or more in order to receive your payout. If you pay this money, you will not receive your £1 million payout. Before playing a lottery online, you should thoroughly check out the company to ensure that they are legitimate. Fraud Watch International lists over 380 lottery scams on its website (see page 194).

Identity theft

Identity theft is where someone gets hold of your personal details and uses them fraudulently to acquire money and goods in your name. You may receive an email telling you that you have won money. To process your claim, you may be asked to send a copy of your driving licence and bank or credit card details. You should also be cautious about giving your credit card details to legitimate online firms with lax security as here it is possible for your credit card details to be stolen.

Unfair software

The software used by the site may be unfair. It may give it a bias that allows it to win the majority of the time. For example, you may be tempted to play roulette. You decide to try out a free game at a site. It appears to be easy to win with the free version. You then try out the game for money but quickly lose. Chances are the free game is rigged to make it appear easy to win and the money game is rigged to make sure you lose more frequently.

Spam

You may open an account with a site and find that your email address has been sold to spammers.

Bonus scams

A site may offer a bonus if you deposit money. Often these bonuses will not be paid. If they *are* credited to your account, they may be deducted from your payout at a later date.

Customer service

Often scam sites will publish customer service contact numbers and an email address appearing to offer 24-hour support. However, if you try to contact them, there will be no answer. Alternatively, a site may be in English but if you have a dispute and phone customer service, the operator speaks a foreign language and no one is available who can speak English. This means that you will have great difficulty getting your dispute resolved.

Phishing

Phishing is a method used to obtain a player's password to their online betting account. What generally happens is that the victim will get an email claiming to be from customer support. It will give some spurious reason why the customer needs to contact them. The victim will be directed to a web page where it will be necessary to type in his user name and password. The cheater then has the information needed to log on to the victim's account, bet with the money in the account and withdraw winnings.

How to protect yourself

You should thoroughly check out an internet betting firm before depositing any money with them. Check that a site is authorized to operate in the country where you are living. Look for a site that has a good reputation. There are lots of gambling forums on the internet where gamblers discuss their experiences about internet betting. Try to get personal recommendations for companies that other people have used without problems. There are also many sites that give blacklists of companies that have failed to pay out or to treat customers fairly. There are some basic checks that you can do. Via an internet search engine perform the following searches, substituting the name of the company for 'company name':

blacklist 'company name'
forum 'company name'
reviews 'company name'
complaints 'company name'.

You will then find out if the company is blacklisted for failing to pay or other scams. By checking gambling forums you can find out what other gamblers are saying about the company. They may not be blacklisted but could, for example, be slow to pay winnings. Be cautious if you find no mention of a company. It could be a new company that has just started in business. Join a gamblers' online discussion group and ask the other members if they have tried out the site you are proposing to bet with.

Ideally, you should look for a site that is government regulated. Some governments have introduced strict controls for sites operating in their countries. You need to ensure that your money is protected and that the sites are fair. UK firms are strictly regulated and licensed. The major UK high street bookmakers have internet sites. Those companies that have built up a solid reputation over the years are more likely to play fair.

Find out where the company is located. If a company is located in a foreign jurisdiction you may have great difficulty in getting your money back if something goes wrong. Be wary if just an email address is given. A legitimate company will display contact information that will include a bricks and mortar address and telephone number. If the firm claims to be a member of a professional association, verify its claim.

You need to ensure that the site has adequate security. In particular, you need to ensure that it is keeping your personal details safe. How safe is your money – is it kept in a 'ringfenced account'. What is its privacy policy – does it divulge information about you to others? Are personal details and payments made over a secure connection? When you give credit or debit card details check that the site is secure. There should be a closed padlock symbol at the bottom of the screen.

Ensure that a site has had its software independently audited by a trustworthy company. You can test out a site's software by playing its free games and seeing if the results are realistic. A quick test is to play roulette for free. Place bets on red for 200 spins and look at the results. There is a 50 per cent chance that red will be spun. If red comes up, for example, 75 per cent of the time, the software cannot be trusted. This casino is trying to give the appearance that it is easy to win.

Look for a site that gives 24-hour support, seven days a week. This ensures that if you have any problems you can contact a member of staff, no matter what time of day it is.

Keep your password secret. Anyone who has access to your password could place bets and withdraw money from your bank account or credit card. If you use a computer that is accessible by more than one person, don't save the password so that it can be automatically entered by the computer. Another person using the computer would be able to access your account.

Keep as little money in your online gambling account as possible. If you get a big win withdraw the money immediately. It is also a good idea to have a separate bank account for your gambling activity. If you do become the victim of a scam, you can keep your losses to a minimum. When you open an account with an online gambling firm, it is also a good idea to open a separate email account. If you start getting spam in this account, you will know that your personal details have been given to spammers. This way you avoid having your personal mailbox full of spam.

Ensure you use a site where personal information is encrypted. As you may be giving personal details, bank account information and credit card numbers to a site, you will want to be sure that this information is securely transmitted and safely held so that it cannot be accessed by a third party.

A card room should have its card shuffling software independently audited to check that it is fair. Ensure that the site actively checks for colluders and has a policy of barring anyone caught. Also, look for a company that has a policy of limiting the number of all-ins. This will stop cheats taking advantage of the all-in rule. Before you deposit money with a company, check it out thoroughly. There are lots of gambling forums on the internet where gamblers discuss their experiences about, for example, online poker. There are also many sites that give blacklists of companies that have failed to pay out or that treat customers unfairly.

If you suspect that you have received a phishing email report it directly to the site. Do not click on any of the links posted in the email. Instead, go directly to the site and log on from the site's home page. Government agencies and online gambling sites are actively working to combat this fraud. The site will often quickly be aware that a fraud of this type is being attempted and will send a warning to members or post a warning on the site.

Disputes

If you have a dispute with an online gambling site there are independent organizations that can help to find a solution. It is a good idea to keep your own records, in case there is a dispute. For example, if you place a bet on a horse race, you should print out a copy of the bet confirmation screen.

Disputes with bookmakers

Do not be afraid to query a bet if you think it has been incorrectly settled. You should initially try to settle your claim with the firm's customer service department. If this fails, and the site is UK based and the bookmaker is a member of IBAS, you can apply to IBAS to settle the dispute.

Call the IBAS number, available 24 hours a day, to request an arbitration form (see page 194 for contact details). Complete the form with all relevant evidence, such as copies of bet receipts. If you are betting over the internet, you should print out the bet confirmation screen. On receipt of the form the service manager will, if he considers it appropriate, refer the dispute to the IBAS panel for adjudication. On completion of the panel's adjudication, both parties will be informed in writing of the decision.

All bookmakers operating within IBAS are registered with the service and have agreed to abide by an IBAS ruling. Any bookmaker registered who fails to fulfil that commitment will be removed from the register. Ninety-five per cent of UK bookmakers are registered with IBAS. You can check on the IBAS website to find if a bookmaker is registered.

Rulings, however, are not enforceable at law.

Be aware that different firms have different rules, so you should always read these thoroughly before placing bets.

Take care if placing large bets as the smaller bookmaking firms tend to have lower maximum payouts.

Always check how many places a firm pays out for each-way and place bets as some are more generous than others.

Common problems

Late bets
Late bets are void. If you get cut off from an internet betting firm, it is up to you to reconnect. For a bet to be valid, it must reach the firm's computer before the off. A bet may appear to leave your computer on time but there can be a delay between its leaving your computer and arriving at the firm's server. It is therefore always advisable to place bets early to ensure that your bet is made.

One event affecting the outcome of another
Be aware that if the outcome on one bet affects the outcome on another, you will get lower odds. For example, if you place an ante-post double (see page 71) on a horse to win the Cheltenham Gold Cup and the Grand National, you will get reduced odds. The bookmaker argues that because the horse won the first race, its odds for winning the second race would be reduced. If you want to place a bet of this type, it is best to negotiate a price with the bookmaker beforehand so you know exactly what your returns will be.

Incorrect odds
Be aware that if odds *look* too good to be true they may be incorrect. Bookmakers' rules give them the right to correct errors in the display or transmission of prices. Bookmakers also have the right to correct errors made by their staff.

Disputes with online casinos and poker sites

If a site is government licensed, you can address any complaints about the site to the licensing authority.

If a firm is a member of the Interactive Gaming Council (IGC), it is possible to apply to this body for mediation.

Disputes with spread betting firms

UK-based spread betting firms are regulated by the Financial Services Authority (FSA). The FSA gives spread betting customers a certain degree of protection. There are regulations governing how they promote their service, for instance. All forms of communication should be clear, fair and not misleading. The firm should make you aware of the risks, which must be explained in the main part of the text and not hidden away in the small print. If it compares its services with those of other firms the comparison must be fair and should not create confusion between itself and its competitors. The firm should include contact details in its communications so that you can ask questions or raise concerns.

If you have a complaint against a firm that you think has not been satisfactorily dealt with by the firm, you have access to the Financial Ombudsman Scheme. In addition, if a spread betting firm goes bust, you have access to the Financial Services Compensation Scheme. The FSA website gives details about how to complain (see taking it further, page 193).

03

before you play

In this chapter you will learn:
- how to set a budget
- how to stay solvent
- about the costs of playing
- how to recognize gambling problems.

Setting a budget

Before you begin gambling, you should work out a financial budget. Calculate all your household and living costs, including savings. Work out how much money you can realistically and comfortably afford to lose – yes, *lose*. Gambling is risky; not everyone wins; there are plenty of losers. You could easily lose all your capital. Be aware that if making money from gambling is your sole intention there are much easier, more profitable and safer ways of doing this.

Once you have decided your budget, make sure you *never* go over this limit. If your personal circumstances change, be sure to recalculate. If you spend only disposable income on gambling, you won't encounter many problems. However, if you start betting with your rent money and lose it, you may be tempted to try to recoup your losses by betting more heavily. This is the route to financial ruin. (See page 22 if your gambling is out of control.)

Additional costs

It's all too easy to go over budget by forgetting to include all the costs. Casino gambling has additional costs that include things such as house advantage, commission and your time. The sites make a charge for the use of their services. Often this charge is hidden by adjusting the odds paid out for winning bets (house advantage). By paying out winning bets at odds lower than the true odds of winning, the site is able to make a profit. The level of house advantage varies with different games and in different online casinos. For example, different versions of roulette have a different house advantage. With single-zero roulette it is 2.7 per cent and with double-zero roulette it is 5.26 per cent. In some games, the charge is more obvious. With card room poker games this charge is in the form of a commission, which is usually a percentage of the pot. This charge is called the rake and is typically 5 per cent of the pot.

Do not aim too high when you are still learning. Even if your budget allows you to play in the more expensive games, stick initially to the cheaper games and gradually work your way up.

Understanding the odds

For a gambler, the term 'odds' has two different meanings, depending on the context in which it is used.

Chances of winning or losing

Before making a bet you will want to know your chances of winning or losing. In this context the 'odds' is a comparison of the chances of winning and losing and is expressed as a ratio. For example, 2 to 1. A shorter way of writing the odds is to put a slash between the two numbers, so 2 to 1 becomes 2/1.

Consider the tossing of a coin. There are two possible outcomes – the coin could land on heads or, just as easily, on tails. Suppose two people, we'll call them A and B, decided to bet on the tossing of a coin. A predicts it will land on heads and B thinks it will land on tails. They each bet £10 and agree that the person predicting the outcome wins the money.

The coin lands on heads so A wins a total of £20 (£10 from B and the £10 he staked) and B loses £10. A has made a £10 profit and B has made a £10 loss. This is gambling in its simplest form. The amount of money that each player risked was £10. This is called the stake. For A there was one chance that he would lose and one chance that he would win. As a ratio this is 1/1 or odds of one to one. Where the odds are 1/1, it is called evens or even money.

This can be applied to any game to find the chances of winning. Suppose A and B were to bet on the throwing of a six-sided die. Here, there are six possible outcomes. Numbers 1, 2, 3, 4, 5 or 6 could be thrown. If A were to bet on throwing a 6, he would have five chances of losing and only one chance of winning (if he threw a 1, 2, 3, 4 or 5 he would lose). The odds against him winning would be 5/1 (five to one).

To calculate the odds in any game, you need to work out how many chances you have of winning and how many of losing.

Winnings compared to stakes

The term 'odds' is also applied to the ratio of winnings compared to stakes. In the coin tossing example, A had the chance of winning £10 for a £10 stake. Expressed as a ratio this is 10/10 or 1/1 (even money). Here, the odds against winning are the same as the odds paid. In other words, the true mathematical odds are being paid.

The odds are quoted as two numbers, for example 2 to 1 and 8 to 1. The number on the left of the odds is the amount won if the number on the right is staked. So, with odds of 2 to 1, if one chip is staked two chips will be won. The player also keeps the stake so in total three chips will be won. For odds of 3 to 2, if 1 chip is staked one and a half chips will be won and the player keeps the stake. Total winnings are two and a half chips. For a five-chip bet on odds of 2 to 1, you simply multiply the odds by 5; so 2 to 1 becomes 10 to 5. For a five-chip bet 10 chips are won and the player keeps the stake giving total winnings of 15 chips.

House advantage

As an example of house advantage, with single-zero roulette the odds paid for a bet on en plein (one number) are 35/1. However, the true odds are 36/1. So, for each spin, the casino has one number working in its favour. The house advantage is 2.7 per cent of the stake. So, for every £37 that you bet, the casino is raking off £1.

The casino comes off even better if the player bets on a roulette wheel with two zeros. Now there are 38 numbers but the odds paid are the same for a winning number (35/1). If a player bets a chip on every number, the casino wins two chips on every spin. By adding an extra zero the casino effectively doubles its profits.

The house advantage varies with different games and casinos. With games such as dice/craps, the type of bet can make a huge impact on the house advantage. Some bets cut the house advantage to under 1 per cent whereas others give the house a massive 16.67 per cent. For some games, such as blackjack, an average is quoted as the house advantage changes throughout the game.

Before you place a bet find out the house advantage, not just for the game as a whole but also for the individual bets. Some bets are simply not worth playing because you are at such a huge disadvantage.

Commission

On some games the casino pays true odds on some of the bets, for example dice and punto banco. However, they charge a commission, which is a percentage of the stake or sometimes a percentage of the winnings.

Games of chance and games of skill

There is a wide choice of betting opportunities online. Gambling can be divided into games of skill where the player can affect the outcome and games of chance where players are relying on luck alone. In general, games where the player has no input are games of chance. These include roulette, dice, big six wheel, straight slots, punto banco and lotteries. Games like poker and blackjack offer players the opportunity to use skill to win. Here players make all the decisions about taking cards. A good knowledge of the game can make the difference between winning and losing. Skill is also involved in betting on horse racing. Here your knowledge of racing can be used to analyse runners' past performances and to predict how they will run in a particular race. With sports betting you can also use your knowledge about past performances to predict who will win. If your intention is to win money, you should concentrate on playing games of skill.

Finding your game

It is a good idea to start off by playing a variety of online gambling games. Then decide which game you like the most and, once you have selected your favourite, concentrate solely on that game.

Check the rules before you start playing

Learn how to play a game before you bet on it. This may seem like common sense, but a lot of people start playing with no understanding of the rules. They end up learning by their mistakes, which can be a costly exercise.

Remember, the rules of gambling games vary enormously. Ensure you fully understand all the rules before you play. Read all the small print on a site. It could save you money in the long run. Whatever game you select, find out as much information about it as possible. If you go on to play the same game on a different site don't assume that the same rules will apply. It may have different ways of playing the games and, furthermore, there may be different payout odds and house advantages.

Learn how to calculate the winnings on your bets

Appreciate your chances of winning.

Many people expect to win but don't realistically assess their chances of winning. With all bets there is the chance that you will lose and it is important to understand how to calculate your chances of winning. You may decide that a bet is simply not worthwhile. Learn how to calculate the odds for the game that you are playing. Before you place a bet, make sure you understand your chances of winning.

With banking games find out both the true odds (your chances of winning) and the odds paid by the casino. Is there a huge difference? You may decide that it is not worth your while having a bet.

Keeping track of money won or lost

Keep a notebook to record details of your online gambling activity. It is very easy to delude yourself into thinking that you do not lose. A record also helps you judge how well you are playing. If your records reveal that you are losing too much, too often, then you can analyse what is going wrong and take measures to reduce losses. Maybe you need more practice. Maybe you need to modify your betting strategy.

If you are gambling in the USA you will find the record useful if you have a big win. In the USA, gambling wins are subject to tax by both the IRS and many state governments. If players win more than $600 on the sports betting, $1200 on slots or $1500 on keno, the casino will notify the IRS. Players may offset gambling losses against winnings, but it is necessary to keep detailed records. The IRS requires players to keep an accurate diary detailing dates, bets made, address of gaming establishment, names of people with you and the amount won or lost. Proof of expenditure like casino receipts and bank records will need to be shown if you are audited.

Know when to stop gambling

It can take an enormous amount of discipline to stop betting, particularly if you are on a winning streak. It is possible to get carried away by the excitement of the game. You may have intended to spend only an hour gambling but you're on a winning streak, so you continue. Because you are betting with your winnings rather than the initial stake money, you decide to place larger bets. Your next best loses, what do you do? For a lot of people, the tendency is to bet more heavily to recoup that loss. This will usually continue until you run out of funds.

Try to decide in advance at what stage you are going to stop betting. Set yourself an amount to win or lose or impose a time limit. Stop playing when you have reached your limit. As soon as a winning streak stops, either bet smaller stakes or stop playing. This approach will minimize your losses.

You should always stop playing if you are tired. You need to ensure that you are concentrating on the game. When you are tired, you take longer to make decisions and are more likely to make mistakes.

It is also wise to avoid alcohol. It tends to slow down your reactions and your ability to think. It also lowers your inhibitions and makes you less likely to care about losses. You should certainly never play if you are drunk.

Staying in control

The majority of gamblers are able to keep to their budgets and bet without its becoming a problem. However, for some people, it can become addictive, leading to financial ruin and family breakdown. If you start losing more than you can afford, seek help.

You can recognize that you have a problem if you:

- view betting as a way of earning money
- continually exceed your budget
- bet money that was intended for living costs
- borrow money for betting
- take days off work to bet
- spend all your free time betting
- find your betting interferes with family life.

There are organizations that can offer solutions. Many have a telephone helpline where you speak to a councillor. They also hold meetings where gamblers can discuss their problems and find solutions. There are also organizations that support gamblers' families. Your general practitioner will also be able to offer advice on counselling. Details of organizations that can help are given at the end of the book.

Some sites also offer self-exclusion schemes. During the period of self-exclusion, they will not take bets from you.

GamCare certification

GamCare is a registered charity that is the UK's national centre for information, advice and practical help regarding the social impact of gambling.

It gives certification to businesses that implement the GamCare Code of Practice for Remote Gambling, which involves implementing the following practices:

- age verification systems
- controls for customer spend
- reality checks within game screens
- self-exclusion options for players
- information about responsible gambling and sources of advice and support
- social responsibility content and sources
- training for customer services in problem gambling and social responsibility.

Details of accredited companies are available on the GamCare website (see taking it further, page 193).

04

card room poker

In this chapter you will learn:
- the history of poker
- basics of poker
- ranking of hands
- about seven-card stud
- about Texas hold 'em
- about Omaha
- playing strategies.

What is online card room poker?

Online card room poker, also referred to as internet poker, is playing poker via a computer connection over the internet. Internet poker firms supply computer software via their websites to connect poker players from all over the world so that they compete against one another in a game. The games can be played 24 hours a day, seven days a week in the privacy of the players' own homes.

All types of poker can be played. Online card rooms offer a variety of games including Texas hold 'em, five-card draw, seven-card stud and Omaha. You can play in live games for money or in free games for fun. There are games at all stake levels starting from £0.01 to no-limit games where you can bet as much as you like. You can also watch games in progress. A wide choice of tournaments is also offered.

For real money games, a rake of typically 5 per cent is charged for the use of the poker room services. The rake is deducted from the winning pot. The rake charged varies with different poker sites. Some offer reduced rates for regular customers. Others may take no rake if, for example, you fold before the flop on Texas hold 'em.

The history of poker

The game of poker first appeared in New Orleans some time during the 18th century. It was particularly popular among the French settlers. The origins of the game are not documented, but it probably evolved from a combination of other card or dice games.

There are several European card games with similarities to poker. These include the French game of poque, the German game of Pochen, the English game of brag and the Italian game of primero. None of these games is a direct descendant of poker but they have most likely had an influence on it. The term flush, for example, comes from primero, which dates from the 16th century. In primero, four cards of the same suit was called a flux, leading to the term flush, which is used in poker to denote a hand of the same suit. The name for poker was probably derived from the French game poque.

A game that has the greatest similarity to poker is the Persian game of as nas, which dates from the 16th century. It was played with a deck of 25 cards with five suits. Each player would initially be dealt two cards. A round of betting would follow. A further two cards were dealt, followed by another round of betting. A fifth card would be dealt, followed by a third round of betting. Hands were ranked in a similar way to poker. The highest ranking hand was five of the same suit (equivalent to a flush in poker) followed by five of a kind. A full house of three of a kind with a pair also features in the ranking. As well as betting the game also allowed players to bluff.

It is also possible that poker was adapted from dice games. Poker is based on the ranking of hands. Dice games with the same principle, the ranking of throws, have been played for at least 2000 years. A Roman dice game called tali is based on the ranking of throws where three of a kind beats a pair, much like poker.

The first written account of poker comes from the diary of Joseph Crowell, an English actor, who was touring America in 1829. He described it as a game where players each received five cards and made bets. The highest combination of cards won.

In 1834, in his book *An Exposure of the Arts and Miseries of Gambling*, Jonathan H. Green gave an account of what he called 'the cheating game'. He saw it being played while on the Mississippi River travelling on a steamboat heading for New Orleans. A deck of 20 cards was used with each player receiving a hand of five. The player with the highest ranking hand would win. The hands were ranked as pairs, three of a kind and four of kind. This early form of poker featured no draws. The players simply received five cards face down and would bet on the cards received.

Along the way, the 20-card deck was replaced by a 32-card deck and, by 1833, a 52-card deck had been introduced. Brief mentions of poker were made in *Hoyles' Games* in 1850 where it was described as a game for 10 players where each player received five cards face down.

New Orleans had numerous gambling establishments where poker was played including the Crescent City House, a luxury casino, which was opened by John Davis in 1827. As America was settled, poker spread and was played on boats that travelled along the Mississippi and Ohio Rivers. Professional gamblers known as sharps made their living by playing cards with riverboat passengers and relieving them of their money. Cheating was rife.

In the USA, poker spread to the west with settlers who travelled on wagon trains. When gold was discovered in California in 1848, gambling flourished in the prospecting camps. San Francisco, which became a huge tented city, had over 1000 gambling houses where gold was the currency. Initially, games like roulette were most popular but gradually card games like poker caught on.

The game spread rapidly during the Civil War (1861–65). Soldiers would play poker to pass the time. Lack of money resulted in their fashioning gaming chips out of flattened bullets and pieces of bone. The soldiers would usually discard their playing cards before battle as playing cards were considered to be 'instruments of the devil' and the soldiers did not want to die carrying them. It was during the Civil War that stud poker first emerged.

Many variations of the game started to appear that could be broadly divided into two types: draw poker and stud poker. In draw poker, all the cards are dealt face down and seen only by the player of the hand. Players are then allowed to exchange cards to improve their hand. In stud poker, some of the cards are dealt face up on the table and players make a hand by combining their cards and those on the table. New rankings of hands and betting methods were also incorporated. In the 1867 edition of *Hoyles' Games*, a straight and a straight flush and an ante had been incorporated into the game. By 1875 jackpot poker and the use of a joker as a wildcard had been mentioned.

Poker players made a living travelling from town to town. Virtually every saloon of the Old West had a poker table where a buckhorn knife would be passed around the table to denote the dealer. This led to the phrase 'passing the buck'. Later, a silver dollar was used, which gave rise to the slang term of a buck for a dollar. Disputes over the game were often settled by gun. One famous poker player from this time was Doc Holliday (1851–87) who on several occasions got into a gunfight over poker.

Poker arrived in England in 1872. It was introduced by Robert C. Schenk, the American ambassador to England. He had been invited to a party at a country house in Somerset where he had taught his fellow guests how to play the game. The hostess persuaded him to write down the rules, which were then published. The game was popular among members of the aristocracy and became know as Schenk poker. Queen Victoria is known to have played the game as a diversion after the death of her husband, Prince Albert.

In 1911 legislation was passed in the United States that prohibited stud poker as it was concluded that it was a game of luck. However, a ruling was also passed that draw poker was a game of skill and therefore not illegal. This led to the decline of stud poker and in new draw games being invented.

Prohibition in the 1920s was responsible for poker becoming a home-based game. With the closure of drinking and gaming establishments, private games were organized and became part of American culture. The traditional venue became the kitchen table where family and friends would gather to play. The playing of private games resulted in many variations appearing, with each household inventing its own rules. New rankings of hands, incorporation of one or more wildcards and different ways of organizing the betting appeared.

When gambling was legalized in Nevada in the 1930s, draw poker was introduced to Las Vegas casinos. In 1970 Benny Binion, owner of the Horseshoe Casino in Las Vegas, decided to hold a poker tournament so that the best players in the world could compete against one another. The tournament, called the World Series of Poker, has become an annual event with players from around the globe competing. The game chosen for the championship was Texas hold 'em – a form of stud poker. This resulted in Texas hold 'em becoming one of the most widely played games.

With the innovation of the internet, online poker came into being. Computer technology allows players from all over the world to compete against one another from the comfort of their own homes. Gaming sites offer traditional poker, video poker and Caribbean stud poker. The first online card room was introduced by Planet Poker in 1998. One year later, Paradise Poker arrived and became the industry leader. Its prominent position was overtaken by Party Poker owned by PartyGaming. It is now the world's largest poker room with over 50 per cent of the online poker market. The site was launched in 2001. It is licensed and regulated by the government of Gibraltar. There are over 70,000 simultaneous players and 8000 tables during peak traffic time each day. The site annually hosts the PartyPoker.com Million, an offline tournament with over $7 million in prizes.

The popularity of online poker is growing year on year. In 2003 there were an estimated 600,000 people playing online. Now it is estimated that over 1.2 million people play internet poker.

Why play online poker?

Poker is a game of skill: the better you are at playing, the greater your chances of winning. Internet poker allows you the convenience of playing in your own home at a time that suits you. There is always a game on, no matter what time of day or night. Many people find playing on the internet less intimidating than playing in a casino. They can remain anonymous to the other players. They are identified only by their pseudonym. There is no need to worry about having a poker face.

Internet poker can work out cheaper than going to a bricks and mortar casino. The rake in an internet casino is just 5 per cent which is lower than many casinos. In addition, you don't have to pay membership fees or travel costs. Neither do you have to worry about a dress code. Via the internet you can play in your pyjamas! Who's to know?

There is a huge amount of competition for customers, which means tax-free betting, low commission rates, initial free bets and bonuses are all offered. It is therefore worth shopping around to find a good deal.

Card room poker

Poker is a gambling game where the aim is to win the pot by having the highest ranking hand. There are many forms of poker, but the games most commonly found in casino card rooms are seven-card stud, Texas hold 'em and omaha.

One deck of 52 cards with the jokers removed is used. A poker hand is made up from five cards. The more difficult a hand is to achieve, the higher its position in the ranking. (Figure 4.1 shows how the hands are ranked.)

The software deals the cards. Before any cards are dealt, players make an initial bet called an ante-bet, or an ante for short. This helps to increase the pot. All the bets are placed in the centre of the table. Instead of making an ante-bet, a round of blind betting may take place. One or more players make a bet before looking at their cards. This is another means of increasing the pot.

The number of cards received varies depending on the game. A number of betting rounds take place. Each player has the option of betting or folding (withdrawing from the game). A player holding a poor hand may decide to fold. If you fold, your cards are returned to the dealer without being revealed to the other players. You lose any bets made. The cards no longer in play are put in a separate pile from the other cards. This pile of folded cards is called the muck pile.

Some games allow players to 'check'. This usually happens on the first round of betting after the cards have been dealt. Instead of betting players announce 'check'. They do not contribute any money to the pot. If they wish to continue in the game they must bet on their next turn. If all the players decide to check, new hands are dealt to everyone.

The first bet determines how much each player has to bet in order to stay in the game. Betting continues clockwise around the table. Each subsequent player must bet at least as much as the previous player to stay in the game. Players may also raise the bet to the maximum. When a bet is raised, players must decide whether or not to match the raise to stay in the game or to fold. As betting progresses more players may fold. If all the other players fold and only one player is left in the game, the remaining player wins the pot. He does not reveal his cards to the other players.

If all players have matched the last bet and there are no further raises a showdown occurs. All remaining players turn their cards face up. The hands of the players are then compared. The player with the highest ranking poker hand wins the pot. In the event of a tie the pot is shared. Figure 4.2 shows example hands. If this were a showdown, player D would win as he has the highest ranking hand.

Standard ranking of hands

The hands are ranked in a set order (see Figure 4.1). Each type of hand is also ranked according to the values of the cards. The highest value cards are aces and the lowest are twos. The cards are ranked in the following descending order: A, K, Q, J, 10, 9, 8, 7, 6, 5, 4, 3, 2. The suits do not affect the ranking, so if two players both have a royal flush, one with hearts and one with spades, the hands will tie.

The highest ranking hand is a royal flush – A, K, Q, J, 10 in the same suit. There are only four ways that this hand can be made, with heart, diamonds, spades or clubs. If you are dealt this hand, you know that you have the highest ranking hand and cannot be beaten by any other player. The only other possibility is that another player may have a royal flush and therefore tie with you.

royal flush

straight flush

four of a kind

full house

flush

straight

three of a kind

two pair

one pair

no pair, highest card

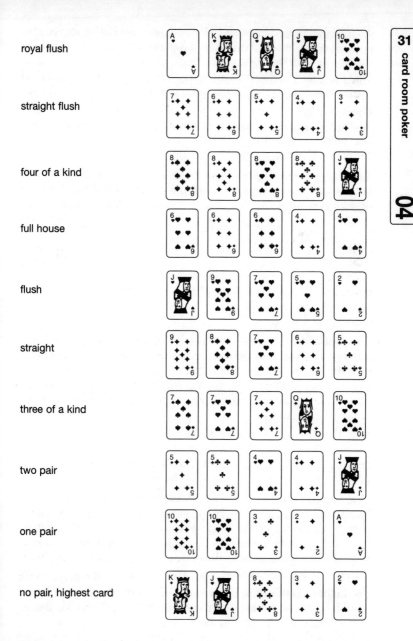

figure 4.1 poker hands ranked from highest to lowest

A straight flush is a run of five cards of the same suit in consecutive numerical order. If two players have a straight flush, the player with the highest card wins so Kc, Qc, Jc, 10c, 9c beats Qh, Jh, 10h, 9h, 8h. If two players both have the same straight flush with different suits, the hand is a tie and the pot is shared.

Four of a kind is four cards of the same numerical value with any other card. Four aces is the highest ranking four of a kind and will beat four kings.

A full house is three of a kind (three cards of the same value) and a pair (two cards of the same value). Where two players have a full house, the hand with the highest value for the three of a kind wins. So 10, 10, 10, 2, 2 would beat 8, 8, 8, A, A.

A flush is a run of five cards of the same suit in any numerical order. Where two players have a flush, the one with the highest card wins. So Js, 8s, 6s, 5s, 3s would beat 9d, 8d, 6d, 5d, 4d.

A straight is five cards of any suit in consecutive numerical order. A, K, Q, J, 10 is the highest straight followed by K, Q, J, 10, 9. Where two players have a straight, the hand with the highest card wins.

Three of a kind, also known as trips, is three cards of the same numerical value with two other cards. 6h, 6d, 6c, 8h, 5d would beat 4d, 4s, 4c, Ad, Kh.

Two pair is two sets of pairs (two cards with the same value) with any other cards. Where two players have two pair, the value of the highest pair decides the winner. A, A, 3, 3, 2 would beat 10, 10, 8, 8, A. If both players have the same two pair, the value of the fifth card decides the winner. K, K, Q, Q, 8 would beat K, K, Q, Q, 4. If two players have exactly the same value cards, there is a tie and the pot is shared.

One pair is two cards of the same value with three other cards of different values. A pair of queens would beat a pair of jacks. If two players have the same pair, the hand with the highest value other cards wins. A, A, 10, 7, 5 would beat A, A, 9, 7, 5. If all the cards are of the same value, there is a tie.

Where none of these hands is held, the winner is the player with the highest card. In a showdown, a hand containing an ace would beat one with a king and so on. Qh, 10h, 7d, 3s, 2c would beat Jd, 10s, 4c, 3h, 2s.

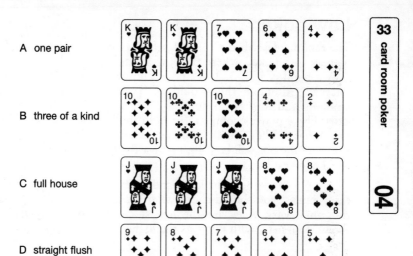

A one pair

B three of a kind

C full house

D straight flush

E straight

F two pair

figure 4.2 example hands

Hand dealt	Number of ways it can be made	Odds against it being dealt in your first hand
Royal flush	4	649,739/1
Straight flush	36	72,192/1
Four of a kind	624	4,164/1
Full house	3,744	693/1
Flush	5,108	508/1
Straight	10,200	254/1
Three of a kind	54,912	46/1
Two pair	123,552	20/1
One pair	1,098,240	15/1
Highest card	1,302,540	1/1

table 4.1 likelihood of being dealt a particular hand in poker

Low poker

The ranking described so far is for high poker. It is also possible to play low poker, where the lowest ranking hand wins. The lowest hand is 5, 4, 3, 2, A and is known as the 'wheel' or the 'bicycle'. Although this would be a straight in high poker, straights and flushes do not exist in low poker. Other games exist where players compete for both the highest hand and the lowest hand. They usually nominate what hand they are playing for. Here the pot will be split, half for the highest hand and half for the lowest hand.

Figure 4.3 shows how the low hands are ranked. Before playing these games, you should check what the lowest rankings are as they may vary. Aces are the lowest card followed by twos, threes, fours etc. with kings as the highest.

Seven-card stud

Each player receives seven cards. The aim is to make the best possible five card poker hand from the seven cards. The player with the best hand wins the pot.

Each player contributes the ante to the pot. Three cards are dealt. Two face down (hole cards), one face up (door card). The first round of betting takes place. The player with the lowest face-up card bets first. This first bet is equivalent to half of the lower stake. If two players have the lowest card, the one with the lower ranking suit bets first. Clubs is lowest followed by diamond, hearts then spades. If, for example, two players have the lowest card with a value of three, one with the three of diamonds and one with the three of spades, the player with the three of diamonds will bet first. Following bets are equal to the lower stake, so in a £1/£2 game, the bet will be £1. Each player may make a maximum of four bets in each betting round.

A fourth card (4th street) is dealt face up, followed by the second round of betting. The player with the highest ranking hand showing bets first. Bets are at the lower stake level.

A fifth card (5th street) is dealt face up, followed by the third round of betting. Bets are at the higher stake level.

A sixth card (6th street) is dealt face up, followed by the fourth round of betting. Bets are at the higher stake level. So in a £1/£2 game, the bets are £2.

the 'wheel'
or 'bicycle'

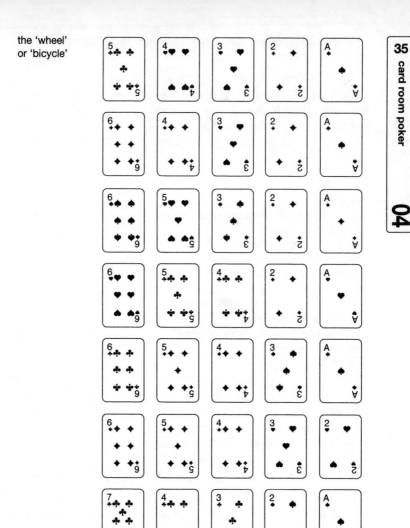

figure 4.3 ranking of hands in low poker

The seventh and final card (river) is dealt face down, followed by the last round of betting.

The showdown then takes place.

The player who bet first on the final round of betting must show her cards first. If the other players have lower hands, they do not have to show their cards.

The player with the highest ranking five-card hand wins.

Summary

Ante bet
Two cards dealt face down and one face up
First betting round
Fourth card dealt face up (4th street)
Second betting round
Fifth card dealt face up (5th street)
Third betting round
Sixth card dealt face up (6th street)
Fourth betting round
Seventh card dealt face down (river)
Final betting round
Showdown

Example

£5/£10, ante £1
There are five players A, B, C, D and E
Ante – each player contributes £1 to the pot

The first three cards are dealt and the players are showing the following:

A has 8
B has ace
C has 7
D has Q
E has 9

First betting round – C has the lowest card so bets first £2.50, D calls, E calls, A calls, B calls.

The fourth card is dealt:

A has 8, 4
B has ace, 3

C has 7, J
D has Q, J
E has 9, 5

Second betting round – B has the highest ranking hand showing so bets first £5. C calls, D calls, E calls, A folds.

The fifth card is dealt:

B has ace, 3, 6
C has 7, J, 9
D has Q, J, Q
E has 9, 5, K

Third betting round – D has the highest ranking hand showing so bets first £10. E folds, B calls, C calls.

The sixth card is dealt.

B has Ace, 3, 6, 2
C has 7, J, 9, 5
D has Q, J, Q, 3

Fourth betting round – D has the highest ranking hand showing so bets first £10. B calls, C calls.

The seventh card is dealt:

B has ace, 3, 6, 2, K
C has 7, J, 9, 5
D has Q, J, Q, 3

Final betting round – D has the highest ranking hand showing so bets first £10. B raises £10 (£20). C calls, D folds.

B's card are ace, ace, ace, 3, 6, 2, K – his best hand is A, A, A, K, 6 – three of a kind.

C has 10, 8, 7, J, 9, 5, K – his best hand is J, 10, 9, 8, 7 – a straight.

C wins.

Seven-card stud strategy

You gradually get more information about each player's hand as the game progresses. At the start of the game you should aim to only play with a good initial hand. Ideally, your lowest card should be equal to or higher than any other card showing. You should play hands that have a good chance of improving to better hands so three of a kind, three cards to a flush, three cards to a straight or a high pair indicate a good start.

If one of the cards you need is showing in another player's hand it is better to fold. For example, you may have an ace in your pocket cards. If an ace is showing in another player's hand, they may well have a pair of aces. This means that your hand has a poor chance of improving.

If you are aiming for a straight, an open ended straight is going to be easier to complete than a closed straight.

If you don't get a good initial hand, folding early will save you money. It is useless progressing all the way to a showdown on the off chance that the other players don't have better hands than you.

Although you may have had a good initial hand, if, after further cards have been dealt, you get nothing to improve your hand and it appears that the other player's hands have improved, you should fold. Staying in until the showdown will be costly. It is better to save your money for a better hand.

Three of a kind will often be good enough to win a hand. If early on you have a high three of a kind, chances are it will be high enough to win on a showdown. In this case, you want to keep everyone betting for as long as possible to maximize the pot. You will need to look out for players who have the possibility of a higher three of a kind or look like they may improve to a straight or higher. In this case you will need to raise to get them to fold. If you have a low three of a kind early on, you will need to try to force out anyone who has the possibility of improving to a higher three of a kind.

Suppose you have three sevens and another player is showing a pair of jacks, you need to force this player out before he improves to three jacks.

You have the advantage when betting from a late position as you can see how everyone else reacts.

Occasionally you will be in a situation when you know that a player can't possibly have their desired hands. For example, two players may each show an ace, but you have the other two aces in your pocket cards. If one of these players folds, the other may try to pull off a bluff and raise early, hoping to convince you that he has three aces. This may be enough to force out the other players, but you know that the best that he can possibly have is a lower pair. Although you have no chance of improving your aces, if the other player gets no decent cards you know that you have most likely beaten him.

Example hands

See Figure 4.4. Suppose you are player A. You have two pair. You can immediately see that player B has a better hand with three of a kind, player C also has two pair, which beats your hand, but could have a full house if he has either another king or another five. In the cards that you are showing, you have the 9, 8 and 7 of hearts. The 10 of hearts and the 5 of hearts are showing in B's and C's hands. This makes it impossible to achieve the straight flush. A straight is a possibility but as three of the tens are shown in B's hand and two of the fives are shown in C's hand this cuts down the chances of making a straight. A would be better off folding this hand. B is showing three of a kind with tens. His best possible hand would be four of a kind followed by a full house. C is showing two pair with kings over fives. His best possible hand would be four of a kind with kings, followed by four of a kind with fives, followed by a full house. C is likely to stay in until the river in the hope of getting either another king or another 5. With no improvement, B will win in a showdown.

figure 4.4 example hands in seven-card stud

Texas hold 'em

Each player receives two cards face down. Five cards are then placed face up in the centre of the table and these community cards are used by all the players. The community cards remain face up on the table. Each player uses any combination of the two cards in his hand and the five community cards to make the best five-card poker hand. At the showdown the players reveal their cards and declare what hand they have.

The deal

Initially, each player receives his two hidden cards followed by a round of betting. The player to the left of the dealer makes the first bet called the small blind, the next player makes the next bet called the big blind. Subsequent players then have the option of calling, raising or folding. Their action will be based on how good they judge their two hidden cards to be. The next three cards are dealt, this is called the flop. These are community cards and are placed face up on the table. Players look at these cards and judge the possible hand that could be made by the end of the game using these cards and their cards. This is followed by another round of betting. A fourth community card is dealt followed by a round of betting. Then the last community card is dealt followed by a round of betting. The first two rounds of betting are at the lower limit and the last two rounds of betting are at the higher limit. Any remaining players then take part in a showdown. The highest ranking hand wins the pot.

Summary

Blind bets placed
Initial deal – two cards face down to each player
First betting round
The flop – three community cards are dealt
Second betting round
The turn – a fourth community card is dealt
Third betting round
The river – the fifth community card is dealt
Final betting round
Showdown

Split pot

Split pots are common in Texas hold 'em. A split pot occurs when both players have the same ranking hand. Suppose player A has Q, J and player B has ace, Q. The board is J, 10, 9, 8, 3.

A has Q, J, 10, 9, 8.
B has Q, J, 10, 9, 8.
The players will share the pot.

Example

There are five players A, B, C, D, E.

A is the dealer
B makes the small blind (£1)
C makes the big blind (£2)
The first two cards are dealt face down. The players look at their cards. C bets £2, D calls, E folds, A raises £2, B calls, C calls, D calls.
The first three community cards are dealt. They are Q, 5, 8.
The second betting round commences.
D bets, A raises, B folds, C calls.
The fourth community card is dealt, the board is now Qh, 5c, 8h, 9h.
The third betting round commences.
D bets, A raises, C raises, D folds, A calls.
The fifth community card is dealt, the board is now Qh, 5c, 8h, 9h, 2d.
A bets, C raises, A calls, C raises, A folds.
C is the winner.

Texas hold 'em strategy

Since you do not get to see the players' pocket cards, the only indication you have of their possible hands is the way in which they are betting.

The number and experience of the players will have an influence on the strategy that you need to use. With a large number of players you need to bear in mind that the competition for a good hand will be greater and there is a greater likelihood that one of the players is going to have a good hand. Where there are lots of players and you have a decent hand you need to try and cut down the competition as early as possible to ensure that those with mediocre hands fold before they get the opportunity to improve. If you are playing with less experienced players they are more likely to stay in the game for longer and not fold. In such games, you need to be certain that you are playing a good hand that has a very good chance in a showdown as you are much more likely to end up in showdowns. In order to make a proper assessment, you really need to see all the community cards first. However, if you always stay in the game until all the community cards have been dealt, in the long run you will lose money. The trick with hold 'em is to learn to fold early when your hand shows little promise and only continue to the showdown with a good hand.

Strategy before the flop

You need to decide whether or not your two cards are worth playing. In general terms it is worthwhile playing any pair, consecutive cards of the same suit, such as 9, 8 or 6, 5 and fairly high cards of the same suit, such as J, 9.

A pair gives you the opportunity to improve to three or four of a kind and opens the possibility to a full house. Consecutive cards of the same suit lead to the possibility of a flush or a straight. High cards of the same suit open the possibility for a flush or a straight.

Strategy after the flop

You now have a better indication of the possible hands. You can assess your position against all the other possibilities, If the community cards have not helped you, they may well have given other players the possibility of a really good hand. If this is the situation then fold now. Suppose you have a pair of fives and the flop gives Ah, Qh, Jh. Chances are that someone has stayed in with an ace or a queen or a jack. Anyone who now has a pair of aces, a pair of queens or a pair of jacks has already beaten your hand. Someone may also now have three aces, three queens or three jacks. Since all the community cards are hearts this opens the possibility of a flush or a straight.

Suppose you have a pair of fives and a flop of 8s, 5c, 2h, you now have three fives. The only danger would come from someone with a three eights. The cards are of different suits so it doesn't help anyone looking for a flush or a straight. You are still in a fairly good position. You now need to eliminate as much competition as possible. Another player may hold a high pair such as two kings or two queens. You need to raise to get them out of the game. If they stay in they could improve to three kings or three queens, which would beat you on a showdown.

Nuts

Occasionally a situation may arise where you know that you have the best possible hand (nuts) that can be made using the community cards. There is no way that you can be beaten. Clearly, in this situation you want to maximize the pot. Your strategy for betting will need to be based on your knowledge of the players. You need to keep the betting at the right level to keep as many of the players betting for as long as possible.

Suppose you have Ah, Jh and the flop is Kh, Qh, 10h, you know at this stage that you have the best possible hand and that no one else can beat you. Chances are someone else will have at least a pair of kings or a pair of queens. You don't need to force anyone out. If doesn't matter how many people stay in until the showdown as you will win it. You have two choices. You can slow play your hand and call until the last betting round. You then raise when you reach the final betting round. Anyone who has paid to get this far will likely want to stay in to the showdown.

Alternatively, you can start raising on the flop. Anyone with a king or a queen will likely stay in with the hope of improving. Anyone with an ace will stay in, hoping to get a straight. They know that there is a possibility of a royal flush but will understand that the chances of anyone making it are rare. If you raise now, chances are they will still stay in to the showdown. The pot that you win will therefore be much greater than a hand that was slow played.

You may not know that you have nuts until all the community cards have been dealt. In example A, the player does not get nuts until all the community cards are dealt. Then he can see that he has the straight Q, J, 10, 9, 8. This is the best possible hand that could be made with the cards shown. A player with, for example, three jacks would lose against him in a showdown. In this game, a number of players may have stayed in. The flop of 4, 2, J was nothing special. Anyone with a high pair would likely stay in. The jack helps the player with Q, 9. The straight needs a 10 and any king or any 8 will complete it. After the next card, the 10 is there. The player now knows that he needs any king or any 8.

In example B, the player has three kings, the best possible hand. The third king comes in the flop. You have two choices you can slow play the hand or start raising. If you slow play you take the risk that anyone with pocket eights or pocket sixes will likely go all the way to the showdown and may get a fourth card on the way. A player with pocket aces is likely to stay in to the river hoping to get another ace. It is therefore a better strategy to start raising. A raise may help to cut the competition. Even if it fails to cut the competition, it will maximize the pot.

A community cards   player's cards

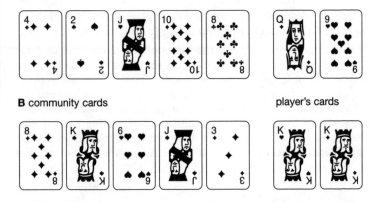

B community cards   player's cards

figure 4.5 'nuts'

community cards

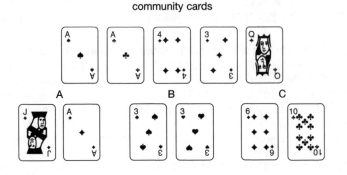

A   B   C

figure 4.6 example hands in hold 'em

Example hands

(See figure 4.6). The best possible hand from the community cards showing is four of a kind with aces, followed by a full house then three of a kind.

Player A will deduce that he has a good hand with three of a kind. He knows that he has the best possible three of a kind and can only be beaten by a full house and since he holds one of the aces, the chances of anyone holding another ace are low. To complete a full house someone would need either two queens, two fours or two threes or to have the other ace with a queen, 4 or 3.

However, player B has a full house. He knows that only four of a kind or a full house with queens or fours could beat him.

Player C has nothing and would be wise to fold.

If player A and B both reach the showdown, B would win.

Texas hold 'em odds

AA	220/1
AK suited	331/1
AK	110/1
Any pair	16/1
Two cards J or higher	10/1
Ace	5.25/1
Two cards suited	3.25/1
Any pair or ace	3.9/1

table 4.2 odds of getting particular pocket cards

Pocket pair to three of a kind on the flop	7/1
Pocket no pair to a pair on the flop	2/1
Pocket AK, A or K by the river	Evens
Two pair on flop to a full house	5/1
Three of a kind on flop to a full house or four of a kind	3/2
Completing a four flush	3/2
Completing open-ended straight flush to flush or straight by river	0.85/1
Completing open-ended straight	2/1
One pair on flop to two pair or three of a kind by river	4/1

table 4.3 odds of improving hands

Odds of getting pocket aces

There are four aces in a deck that can be dealt in six different ways to make a pair of aces.

The four aces can be dealt in six ways.

$$\frac{4 \times 3}{1 \times 2} = 6$$

From 52 cards, 1326 two-card hands can be dealt:

$$\frac{52 \times 51}{1 \times 2} = 1326$$

1326/6 = 221. The odds of getting pocket aces are therefore 220/1.

Odds of getting any pair

There are 13 possible pairs and each pair can be dealt in six ways.

$$1326/(13 \times 6) = 17$$

The odds of getting any pair are 16/1.

Calculating the odds of improving on your hand

Suppose you have a pair of queens and you want to calculate the odds of getting a third queen on the flop, there are two queens and 48 other cards in the deck. There are three cards dealt in the flop, giving you three chances to get a queen. Your odds of getting a queen are 7/1:

$$(52 - 2 - 2)/48 \times 3 = 8$$

The odds, therefore, are 7/1.

Omaha

Each player receives four cards face down. Five cards are then placed face up in the centre of the table to be used by all the players. Each player uses any two cards in his hand and three of the community cards to make the best five-card poker hand. Only two of the players hole cards can be part of the five card poker hand. The game is dealt in a similar way to Texas hold 'em with a flop of three cards and blind bets. What makes the game more complicated is the way in which the five-card poker hand is made. When you see the cards you need to give some thought as to what hand you have actually got. At first glance, you may seem to have an exceptionally good hand. But you need to remember that you can only use two of your hole cards (see Figure 4.7).

By looking at the cards in total, player A can immediately see a full house (three fours and two tens). However, because only two cards can be used from his hand he only has two pair (two tens and two fours).

Player B appears to have a straight (S, K, Q, J, 10) but the hand actually held is two pair (two jacks and two tens).

At first glance, player C may appear to have a full house (three twos and two tens). However, he may only use two cards from his hand so only holds two pairs (two tens and two twos).

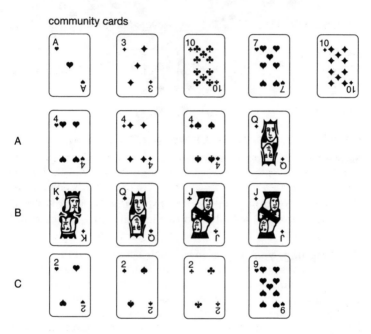

figure 4.7 example hands in Omaha

Omaha strategy

The strategy is similar to that of Texas hold 'em. You really need to see the flop before you can make any decision. However, a situation can arise when it is wise to fold immediately after you have been dealt your hole cards.

Being dealt four of a kind in your hole cards is one of the worst possible situations. You can only use two cards so at best you have a pair with no chance of improving on them. Being dealt three of a kind also fives you only a remote chance that the fourth card will appear in the community cards. The same is true of being dealt four cards to a possible flush; your chances of making the flush are drastically reduced.

figure 4.8 hands to fold on in Omaha

The best cards to play with are high pairs or high cards of the same suit (if you hold only two of the same suit), which could lead to a flush.

After the flop, you will be in a much better position to judge your chances of winning. Then you can assess all the possibilities and work out your chances of making a good hand. It is at this stage that you need to force out anyone who has the potential to improve his or her hand into one that could beat yours.

Nuts

As with Texas hold 'em, occasionally a situation may arise where you know that you have the best possible hand (nuts) that can be made using the community cards. There is no way that you can be beaten. Clearly, in this situation, you want to maximize the pot. Your strategy for betting will need to be based on your knowledge of the players. You need to keep betting at the right level to keep as many players betting as possible.

Understanding the odds

In standard games of poker, 52 cards are used to make five-card hands. There are 2,598,960 different possible hands that can be dealt:

$$\frac{52 \times 52 \times 50 \times 49 \times 48}{1 \times 2 \times 3 \times 4 \times 5} = 2,598,960$$

To appreciate just how rare the higher ranking hands are, when only five cards are dealt consider how long it takes to play 649,740 hands (the chances of getting a royal flush). If you play, for example, an average of one hand every five minutes, you would need to continue playing constantly for approximately six years and two months! By playing for a few hours each week the chances of being dealt a royal flush in your first hand are nothing short of a miracle.

Take a pack of cards and deal them out into five card poker hands. By continually repeating this you will begin to appreciate just how rare it is to be dealt one of the higher ranking hands. You will start to get some idea about which hands are worth playing. Pairs are very common. Pairs appear very low down in the ranking but a high pair can often be sufficient to win a game like five-card stud.

If poker is played with only five cards and no further cards exchanged for others from the pack, players are mostly competing with low ranking hands. This is one of the main reasons why so many variations of poker exist. By increasing the number of cards dealt to each player or allowing players to exchange some of the cards for new ones from the pack, the chances of having a higher ranking hand are increased. The varied games add more interest and excitement.

How the odds change with different games

Poker can be played in a wide variety of ways. A different number of cards may be dealt and the number of cards players can exchange may vary. To have a good knowledge of the odds for your particular game you need to take these factors into consideration in your calculations.

In games like seven-card stud and Texas hold 'em, a five-card poker hand is made from seven cards. With seven cards you are able to make up 21 different five card poker hands:

$$\frac{7 \times 6 \times 5 \times 4 \times 3}{1 \times 2 \times 3 \times 4 \times 5} = 21$$

This hugely improves each player's chances of achieving a higher ranking hand. By looking at the cards that each player is showing, or the community cards, you can deduce the possible hand that they may hold and calculate the chances of their having that particular hand.

With Omaha, nine cards are used to make a five-card poker hand. Therefore, 60 different five card poker hands can be made by each player, which makes it even easier to achieve a high ranking poker hand.

Therefore, note that a pair of aces may have been enough to win a game of five card stud, but in omaha, a pair of aces is highly likely to be beaten.

You are also able to adjust any calculations about players' hands by taking into account the cards that you hold and those that the other players have on display. Consider a game of seven-card stud, where four cards of each player's hand are displayed.

A player may have two queens and two jacks displayed. In order to make a full house, he needs either another jack or another queen in his hand. If you have a queen in your hand and another player has a jack displayed, then a full house with queens and jacks can only be made from two other cards, the remaining jack or queen.

If there are five players, 20 cards are displayed and you also have three cards in your hand. That leaves 29 other cards. Two cards would five a full house. This means that the player has odds of 15.5/1 against having a full house $(29 - 2)/2 = 13.5/1$.

If no jacks or queens were displayed by other players or in your hand, the odds against his having a full house with jacks and queens would be $(29 - 4) / 4 = 6.25/1$. You can see that taking into account the cards held by you or displayed by other players can make a big difference to the odds.

Pot odds

The pot odds is the odds that you are getting for making a bet. For example, if there is £50 in the pot and you need to make a bet of £5 to stay in the game, you are getting odds of 10/1.

By comparing the odds to achieve a particular hand, with pot odds you can decide whether or not it is worthwhile making a bet.

To make a bet worthwhile, the pot odds would need to be higher than the odds of achieving a winning hand. Suppose the pot odds are 10/1 and the odds of your making a hand that you assess is sufficient to win are 4/1, it is worthwhile betting. If, however, the pot odds are 8/1 and the odds of your achieving a winning hand are 14/1, then it not worthwhile betting.

Calculating percentage chance of improving

To simplify the arithmetic, there is an easy calculation to make that is the approximate percentage chance of improving your hand. You first need to know how many cards can complete your hand (outs). You then double this number and add 2.

Example

With Omaha, if your pocket cards are two spades and the flop gives two spades, you have a chance of making a flush with spades. There are 13 spades in total. Four of them have been dealt, two to your hand and two to the flop. There are nine left in the deck ($13 - 4 = 9$).

This gives you nine outs: $(9 \times 2) + 2 = 20$.

You therefore have approximately a 20 per cent chance of making the flush. Your bet should be no more than 20 per cent of the pot value. If there is £200 in the pot, for example, your bet should be less than £40 to be worthwhile.

Example

You have a pair of kings and want to calculate your chances of getting a third king. There are four kings, you have two, which leaves two in the deck. You therefore have two outs: $(2 \times 2) + 2 = 6$.

You therefore have approximately a 6 per cent chance of making the three of a kind. Your bet should be no more than 6 per cent of the pot value. If there is £100 in the pot, your bet should be less than £6 to be worthwhile. If you need, for example, to bet £10 to stay in the game, it would be better to fold.

Bluffing

What is bluffing?

If all the other players fold in a game of poker, the remaining player wins the pot and does not have to reveal the cards held to the other players. This means that it is possible to win a game without necessarily having the best hand. Bluffing is convincing the other players that you have a good hand when you actually have quite a poor hand. Bluffing is achieved by placing a big bet to intimidate the other players to fold. The advantage of bluffing is that it allows you to attempt to win a pot even when the cards that you have are poor in value and would have little chance of winning in a showdown. To succeed with a bluff you need to raise the betting to a level high enough to ensure that the players fold before the game reaches a showdown. If your bluff is successful you will win the pot and no one will know that you were bluffing. If, however, you are forced into a showdown, you must reveal your cards and your bluff will have failed.

Semi-bluffing is making a big bet when your current hand is poor but has a good opportunity to improve. Your initial cards may not be enough to win a game but if you stay in until more cards are revealed you may get what you want to make a great hand. If you don't get the cards you want then you continue to play out the hand as if they are there. In Texas hold 'em, you may, for example, have two cards for a potential straight or flush. After the flop, you still need two cards to make a straight. You continue playing as if the flop gave you what you needed for a good hand. By sufficiently raising the stakes you attempt to make the others fold. If this does not work, you continue to bet and hope that you get your necessary cards.

When should you bluff?

Bluffing is most effective in high stake games where it is possible to substantially increase bets. If it becomes expensive for a player to stay in a game they are more likely to consider folding. Bluffing is particularly suited to no-limit Texas hold 'em, because you can bet what you like: you can make a huge bet that is big enough to make anyone think twice before continuing to play.

The size of the pot will influence your decision on whether or not to bluff. Bluffing is most useful for taking small pots. In a situation where lots of players have folded, you are left with little competition for the pot. With a small pot, players are more likely to fold if they have a mediocre hand. Although they could improve, they will often prefer to sit the game out and wait for a better hand with a bigger pot. In contrast, a large pot will be much more competitive. Players will be more likely to fight for a pot where they have contributed a substantial stake.

Bluffing is best used against good players. A good player will realize that your increase in stakes means that you either have a good hand or that you are bluffing. If you have a reputation as a tight player, the increase in stakes will be taken seriously.

Bluffing will not always work. Not every player will back down, particularly if they believe that they have a good hand. If you find yourself in the situation where your bluff is not believed, it may be better to fold earlier rather than later. If you are continually re-raised you can quickly lose all your chips.

Ideally, you should bluff when there are just a few people left in the game. It is easier to convince one or two people that you have a good hand rather than having to convince five or six.

Your position in relation to the dealer will have an influence on whether or not it is worthwhile to bluff. It is not good to bluff from an early position as you have no idea if the other players have been dealt a good hand or not. It is much better to bluff from a late position as you will see players' reactions to their hands and how they bet.

A good time to bluff is when you have just won a big pot with a good hand. A forceful round of betting will be more likely to convince the other players that your luck is in and you've got another good hand.

It's important not to get caught bluffing as this will cause you to lose credibility. You need to be able to force players to fold without getting caught in a showdown. If you've recently been caught bluffing, players will tend to call your bets. You can, however, use getting caught to your advantage if shortly after you have a good hand. The other players will remember that you just bluffed and are more likely to assume that you are trying to pull off another bluff. You can then use this opportunity to raise your stakes and take a big pot.

You should bluff when other players are running short on chips. They are more likely to fold in order to play in the next game. You will need to take care if they stay in though, as if they go all in, you will be forced to a showdown. Avoid bluffing against players with lots of chips as they are more likely to carry on betting.

Bluffs that seem to represent a specific hand like a flush, straight or full house have a much better chance of succeeding. Trying to convince the other players that you have a good hand will be easier. If there appears to be nothing on the board it will be harder to convince the other players that you have anything special.

A bluff when you are on a losing streak or when you are low on chips comes across as desperation and is less likely to be believed by the other players. If you have to go all in, you will be forced to a showdown and your bluff will be revealed, which will reduce your credibility.

Be wary of bluffing when there are high cards in the flop like A, K, Q, J or 10 as someone will inevitably have a match and will be highly unlikely to back down. If there is an ace in the flop, there is bound to be someone who already has an ace in their hand.

For example, with a flop of A, K, J anyone holding an ace, king or jack will stay in, anyone with a pair of aces, pair of kings or pair of jacks will stay in. So too will anyone holding a queen with the hope of getting a straight. The competition for the pot will be too great. If the board ends up as A, K, J, 10, 7, anyone with a queen knows that they have nuts. Anyone with three of a kind will likely stay in. Anyone with an ace and another high card may also stay in. Those that have just missed their hand may also stay in and attempt a bluff.

If there are low cards in the flop, it is less likely that someone will have a match. Players are much more likely to stay in with high cards. If you start betting strongly as if you have a three of a kind or a high pair this is more likely to be believed. You need to ensure that you bet strongly enough to force out your opponents before more cards are dealt.

If you bet pre-flop and didn't get the desired hand after the flop, you continue betting as if you got what you wanted. The players will note your strong position pre-flop and your apparently stronger position post-flop.

Keep an eye on the players who have folded as they will inevitably show that they threw away a good hand. If they had a matching pair in their hand, it diminishes the chances that the other players have a good hand.

Get plenty of practice

You need to be able to correctly identify a poker hand and recognize immediately the value of your hand and where it comes in the ranking. When you first look at your cards, they may appear to show nothing, they will be in a random order and it may not be at first obvious that you have, for example, a straight or a possibility of a straight. At the showdown, you will need to know, for example, that your full house beats a flush.

To get better at recognizing the hands you can practise assessing the hands by dealing out dummy hands. Deal out hands of five cards, identify the poker hands and put them in the correct ranking order. You will soon appreciate how infrequently a good hand is dealt. Once you have mastered the ranking, you can then start to judge whether or not a hand is worth playing.

Get plenty of practice. Take a pack of cards and deal out dummy hands as if you're playing the game with several players. Look at your own hand. Decide whether or not it is worth playing. Then assess your hand against the others. Did you make a good decision? Would any of the other hands have beaten yours? Are you throwing away hands that could easily win? By continuing to do this you will learn the sort of hands that are worthwhile playing and those that are not.

Play alone or with friends until you are familiar with all situations. Practise placing bets as you play. Some games are played so quickly that it can be difficult for a novice to follow them. With practice you will become faster.

As mentioned earlier, it is important to play at the right level. Don't aim too high when you are still learning. Stick to the simpler, cheaper games and gradually work your way up. Remember, the higher the stakes the better the players.

How online poker works

Online card rooms use computer software to produce virtual card rooms. Players see a depiction of a card table on their screen, showing the other players (cartoon style) and details of their own hand much like you see on console games.

The software uses a random number generator to determine the order of the deck of cards. This ensures that, with each game, the cards are randomly shuffled. The software deals the cards and prompts the players to make decisions about their hands. At the appropriate times in the games it gives the options of check, call, bet, raise or fold. These options will appear on the screen. Players select which option they want by clicking with their computer mouse. The screen will tell you how much you need to bet to stay in the game and provide the options that you have at that point in the game. Throughout the game, a running total of the pot and the actions of the other players are shown. At the showdown, the cards of the remaining players will be revealed. The software deducts the amount of the bets from the player's account and credits any winning pots to their account.

Because the games are operated by a computer they are run at a much faster pace than normal poker games. There is no dealer so no time is wasted while the cards are shuffled, dealt and collected. There is often a time limit imposed. If you do not act within the time limit, your hand is folded.

The rules tend to be similar to those found in bricks and mortar casinos. Due to the internet environment, there are special rules that cover what happens if a player gets cut off from the internet during a game (see later).

Cards are burnt as in a normal poker game. You don't see the cards getting burnt. The players take it in turn to be the dealer. They don't physically deal the cards themselves. All the dealing is carried out by the software. A disc (dealer button) will indicate which player is the current dealer.

Once all the cards are dealt, the various options that are available during the game will appear on the screen – raise, call, check and fold. The first player has one of three choices: check, bet or fold. Once a bet has been placed, the subsequent players must call, raise or fold. In draw poker you will need to select the cards you want to hold.

Players can take a break, leaving the game for a short while and returning to the same table.

Joining a game

To begin playing you will need to log on to your account. This will take you to the lobby. Here you will find a list of all the games currently in progress. If there is an empty seat at a table you click on 'Join game' and you will be taken to that game. If there are no empty seats available, you can put your name on a waiting list. You can specify what stakes you want to play for and how many people you want to play against.

For each table there will be details of how many players are currently sitting at the table and how many are on the waiting list. If you put your name on the waiting list, you will be notified when a place becomes available.

You may sit in any chair that is available. You will be shown the players' nicknames and how much money they are playing with.

An information box will tell you the name of the game, the limits and type of game the blinds, ante and the buy-in.

When you first sit down at a table you are prompted to enter the amount of your buy-in. There will be a minimum buy-in that will depend on the game being played.

Take your time to familiarize yourself with the layout as they differ with different sites. Most sites allow you to customize the screen to suit your taste.

Watch the games before playing and only join once you are confident that you understand exactly what you need to do. Read the terms and conditions before agreeing to them. Many sites have a code of conduct.

What happens if you get disconnected from the internet?

If you get disconnected from the internet while a game is in progress, the way that your hand is treated will vary with different sites so you should carefully check the rules. In general, your hand will automatically be played as all in. If check is an option, the system will check for you. If not you will go all in and a separate pot will be created. If you have the winning hand, you will be awarded the pot that built up at the time that you were disconnected. To avoid abuse of this feature, players are limited to a number of all ins in a 24-hour period. If you exceed the number of all ins in that time, your hand will be automatically folded if you get cut off from the internet.

Chatting to other players

Players can chat to each other during play by typing messages from their keyboards. There are restrictions on what you can say. It is forbidden to talk about what is in your hand during a game. Even after you have folded you must not tell other players what you had in your hand until the game is completed. Giving away information about your hand during a game helps the other players to make decisions. You may chat freely once a game has finished. To save time and typing out long sentences, abbreviations are used while chatting. Some of the abbreviation used are shown in the following box. Offensive language is not allowed and writing in capitals or using exclamation marks makes you appear to be shouting.

Chat terms

brb – be right back
gg – good game
gh – good hand
gp – good play
gtg – got to go
hehe – very amusing
lol – laugh out loud
nh – nice hand
omg – oh my god
tx – thanks
ty – thankyou
vnh – very nice hand
wb – welcome back
wp – well played
wtg – way to go

Cheating

Combating cheating has always been a priority for online poker firms. Online poker is vulnerable to *collusion*. With online poker, because you can't see the other players, you can communicate your hand to another player. It is easy for two players who are friends to communicate while playing either over the phone or via instant messaging. If the two decide to collude, whichever player has the better hand plays it and the other folds. This way, they have two chances of getting a better hand. If more players cooperate as a team, then the victim stands little chance of winning.

It would also be possible for a computer expert to operate a number of computers consecutively and make it appear that several players are competing against one another when, in fact, all the computers are in one room and he is controlling the action of all the players bar one in a game. In this situation, as he knows all the hands except that of one opponent, he can play in such a way that the highest ranking hand always wins.

The online poker rooms are aware of this form of cheating and combat it using software to detect colluders. The software monitors the frequency of two players playing in the same game, unusually high winning rates and suspicious playing patterns like players folding when they have very good hands. If colluders are caught they will have their accounts suspended and may lose any money held in their accounts. Their membership to the poker room will be cancelled and details of their cheating may be shared with other gambling sites, which will make it more difficult for them to open another account with a poker room. If you suspect that this kind of cheating has occurred in a game that you have been involved in, you should inform the site.

All-in abuse

Some players will abuse the all-in rule. They will disconnect their computer at a time when it is advantageous to do so. To combat this sites place limits on the number of times that all-in can be used. If the player is disconnected again then their hand is automatically folded.

Playing strategy

There is no physical contact between the players. You cannot see them and they cannot see you. This means you do not have to worry about keeping a poker face and paying attention to your body language. This also means that you cannot assess other players' body language and look for tells. As technology improves, games may be introduced where the players can see each other via web cameras.

As you cannot see the players you need to develop a different strategy for playing. The strategy used needs to be based more on probabilities, betting patterns and knowledge gained from previous games with players that you may encounter in the future. If you regularly play on the same site, you may regularly play with the same players and build up a body of information about the habits and betting patterns of these players.

Internet tournaments

Online card rooms offer lots of poker tournaments. Internet tournaments are much shorter than traditional tournaments.

Single-table tournaments are where nine players compete. There is usually a prize for the top three finishers with the prize being divided as follows:

winner 50%
second place 30%
third place 20%

In multi-table tournaments, you will compete against hundreds of other players. The players will be randomly located seats and may play several rounds. As players get knocked out, the remaining players are re-seated until just nine players remain on the final table. The winner is the player who wins all the other players' chips. The advantage of multi-table tournaments is that you can win a large prize for a small entry fee.

Speed tournaments

With speed tournaments, the value of the blind increases every few minutes. This ensures that the tournament is quickly finished. Speed tournaments can be played both as single table games and multi-table games.

05

**horse racing
and sports
betting**

In this chapter you will learn:
- about types of online betting
- how to bet
- about the advantages and
  disadvantages
- how to play it safe.

Types of online betting

There are several different types of site that take bets on horse racing, greyhound racing, sports and other events. These are bookmakers, betting exchanges and spread betting firms. All offer different ways of betting.

Bookmakers

Online bookmakers accept bets at fixed odds on a huge range of events including horse racing, greyhound racing, sports and election results. The betting opportunities are similar to those offered by on-course and off-course bookmakers. The range of bets available include single, multiple, each way, forecast and tricast bets.

For horse racing at the bookmaker's website, you can find details of the race cards, prices, ratings, naps, form and statistics. Live commentaries of the races are given. The services are offered in a number of languages and bets can be made in a choice of currencies. Minimum stakes vary but can be as low as 1p. Maximum stakes and payouts vary from bookmaker to bookmaker so you should check the rules if you intend to make large bets. Many bookmakers also provide an online bet calculator so that you can easily work out your payout. Some bookmakers also give you the opportunity to see the odds as fractions or as decimals. This makes it easier to compare prices with betting exchanges (see later). The bookmakers also provide price alerts that can be sent to you via email or mobile phone so that you can keep track of any changes.

Like a traditional bookmaker, there is a profit for the firm built into the prices of around 17 per cent.

How prices are determined

A bookmaker uses an expert called a handicapper to assess the chances of each runner in the race. The handicapper will consider a number of factors to determine the chances of each horse. Things like pedigree, recent performance, the jockey, weight carried and the condition of the ground will be taken into account. A book of prices is then made depending on the assessment. The runner that he thinks is most likely to win will have the lowest price and is called the favourite. Occasionally, two runners are deemed to have an equal chance of winning. They will have the same price and be called joint favourites. If several runners have the same lowest price, they are called co-favourites.

The prices of the horses in a race can vary enormously. Just because a horse has a large price it does not mean that it will not win. In 1990 Equinoctial won at Kelso at a price of 250/1 – the longest odds recorded in British horse racing.

The initial prices offered are called tissue prices. This is just a preliminary indication of the prices and they tend to be a conservative estimate of a horse's chance of winning. Once bets have been made the prices are said to have been layed. This means a betting market has been made. The prices then change depending on how much money is bet. The prices do not show the chances that a horse has of winning. Instead, they reflect how much money has been bet on them. The horse attracting the greatest amount of money in bets will have the lowest price. The horse attracting the least amount of money will have the highest price. Horses with high prices are called outsiders or rags.

Bar

When prices are quoted for a race, the odds for some outsiders may not be given. Instead, a bar price is shown. This means that all the horses not quoted in the betting are at a higher price than that given in the bar. For example, in a 10-runner race, prices may be given for seven of the runners and a bar price of 25/1. This means that the other three horses all have a price of greater than 25/1. If you want to place a bet on one of the unquoted horses, you will need to agree a price with the bookmaker.

Understanding the odds

When you go to place a bet, you will see that there are prices (odds) quoted for the runners. These prices are usually made up of two numbers with a slash between, for example 5/4, 11/8, 5/1, 7/2, 15/2, 25/1. These prices are a ratio telling you what you will win for a particular stake. The amount on the left of the price is what you will win if you bet the amount on the right. The money bet is called the stake. If you win, your stake is refunded. The total amount won is called the returns or payout.

Example

If the price quoted is 6/1, you will win £6 for every £1 staked. Your stake is also refunded. If you bet £5 on a horse at 6/1, your returns will be (6 x 5) + 5 = £35.

If you bet of £4 on a horse at odds of 6/4, your returns will be 6 + 4 = £10.

If you bet £1 on a horse at odd of 11/2 will return 5.5 + 1 = £6.50.

Odds against and odds on

Where the number on the left of the price is bigger than the number on the right the term odds against is used; where it is less it is called odds on. Where both numbers are the same, e.g. 1/1, the term even money or evens is used.

Example

1/1 is even money (always written as 'evens')

13/8 is odds against, 8/13 is odds on

5/2 is odds against, 2/5 is odds on

You will often hear prices quoted with the word 'on', for example, '2/1 on'. This actually means that the price is 1/2. Therefore, when the word 'on' is quoted, to find the correct price the order of the price needs to be reversed: 11/8 on is 8/11, 7/4 on is 4/7 and 6/5 on is 5/6. This can lead to confusion, particularly if you mishear.

Each way

Bookmakers also accept each-way bets. This is two bets. One bet is for the horse to win the race and the other is for it to be placed second, third or fourth. The number of places paid depends on the number of runners in the race. (See Table 5.3.) It is important to pay particular attention to the number of places paid as some bookmakers offer lower odds than others.

If your horse wins the race, one bet will be settled at the full odds but the other bet will be settled at a fraction of the odds.

Suppose you bet £10 each way on a horse. Your stake will be £20 because an each-way bet is two bets. If the horse wins at 4/1 and one-quarter of the odds are paid for the place:

- The win part of the bet pays (4 × 10) + 10 = £50.
- The place part of the bet pays only one-quarter the odds of the win; to find the correct odds to calculate the returns you need to multiply the number on the right of the price by four. (If the bet was at 1/5 odds you would need to multiply by five.)
- So the win odds of 4/1 become place odds of 4/4 (which is evens − 1/1). So the place part pays (1 × 10) + 10 = £20.
- Total returns are £50 + £20 = £70.
- If the horse were to come second, the win bet would be lost but the place bet would be won. The returns would be £20.
- In races where there are four runners or less, it is not possible to bet each way. It is only possible to bet on the winner. If an each-way bet is placed, all the stakes go on the horse to win. This is called all up and is often abbreviated to AU.

Factors affecting prices

Even though you may have taken a price, the odds at which your bet is settled may be adjusted if certain conditions apply.

Non-runners

A non-runner is a horse that does not take part in the race. A horse may be withdrawn any time up to the off of a race. If you bet on a non-runner on the day of the race, your stake will be refunded. If, however, you bet ante-post, you will lose your stake.

If a horse comes under starter's orders in a race but refuses to run, it is not considered a non-runner. It is important to check the results because a horse can be withdrawn right up to the last minute. You may see it set off for the start, but it may, for example, be withdrawn because it refuses to go into the starting stalls.

Withdrawn horses

Rule 4 deductions

After a book has been made on a race, a horse may be withdrawn. This will mean that the prices offered on the race will be incorrect, as they would have been worked out including the withdrawn horse. The bookmakers are therefore allowed to make an adjustment to the prices, called a rule 4 deduction (usually abbreviated to R4). The deduction is quoted as an amount in the pound, for example 10p in the £. The amount of the deduction is determined by the price of the withdrawn horse (see Table 5.1). The deduction applies to both winning and placed horses. Only the winnings are affected and not your stake.

Odds of horse withdrawn		Deduction	% of winnings
3/10 or shorter		75p in £	75
Over 3/10	up to and including 2/5	70p in £	70
Over 2/5	up to and including 8/15	65p in £	65
Over 8/15	up to and including 8/13	60p in £	60
Over 8/13	up to and including 4/5	55p in £	55
Over 4/5	up to and including 20/21	50p in £	50
Over 20/21	up to and including 6/5	45p in £	45
Over 6/5	up to and including 6/4	40p in £	40
Over 6/4	up to and including 7/4	35p in £	35
Over 7/4	up to and including 9/4	30p in £	30
Over 9/4	up to and including 3/1	25p in £	25
Over 3/1	up to and including 4/1	20p in £	20
Over 4/1	up to and including 11/2	15p in £	15
Over 11/2	up to and including 9/1	10p in £	10
Over 9/1	up to and including 14/1	5p in £	5
Over 14/1		no deduction	

table 5.1 rule 4 deductions

Example

A horse that was 4/1 in the betting is withdrawn. The SP of the winning horse is 2/1. The price will be subject to a rule 4 deduction of 20p in the £.

A £10 bet tax paid on a winning horse at 2/1 would normally return £30. With a rule 4 deduction of 20p in the £, the bet would return £26.

Calculation: (20 − 20%) + 10 = 26

If there is sufficient time before the race is off, a new book will be made. In this case, the rule 4 deduction will apply to prices taken before the time that the new book was made. Prices taken on the new book and SP prices will not be subject to a rule 4 deduction.

Each way bets

Horses being withdrawn can also affect the odds paid and the number of places paid for each-way bets. When you placed your bet there may have been eight runners, meaning you would expect to be paid if your horse came third. However, if a horse is withdrawn, the third-placed horse no longer counts, as there will only be seven runners. You will only get paid if your horse is first or second.

Dead heats

Occasionally two horses or more are declared the winner. This is termed a dead heat. When a horse dead heats for first place, the returns are halved. If there are three horses in the dead heat, then the returns are divided by three. If placed horses dead heat, the returns are only reduced if there are more places than usual being paid. For example, if two horses dead heat for second place and three places would normally be paid, the returns will not be affected. If, however, only two places would normally be paid and two horses dead heat for second place, the returns of the placed horses will be affected. So too will the returns of any each-way bets on the winner.

Types of price

Ante-post prices

When a bet is placed before the day of the event it is called an ante-post bet. For major races like the Grand National and the Derby, prices are available many months before they are run. The prices are normally more favourable than those offered on the day of the event. However, if your runner is withdrawn from the race, your stake is automatically lost.

Sometimes there are too many horses entered for a race. For safety reasons, only a certain number may run. In this situation a procedure called balloting out will determine which horses run. If your runner is balloted out, your stakes will be refunded. The prices of the remaining horses will be adjusted according to rule 4 (see page 66).

Although ante-post betting has its risks, such as horses being withdrawn, the benefit of the higher prices is usually advantageous to the punter.

Early morning prices

Most bookmakers offer early prices on several races. These are usually on the handicap races but some may give prices on all the races. These prices are quite often advertised in the sporting press. It is worthwhile comparing the prices offered by different operators, as they will vary.

As soon as betting starts on the race the prices will change. Some bookmakers will allow customers to take the advertised price up to a certain time limit. Some also guarantee that if their early morning prices are worse than the starting prices, the bet will be settled at the starting price. If you want to take the early morning prices, you should place your bet as early as possible. The prices will only be available up to the first show (see board prices/shows).

The races will be running the same day, so if your selection does not run, your stake will be refunded.

Board prices/shows

Around 10 minutes before the race starts, prices will be passed from the racecourse. The prices represent an average of what the bookmakers on the course are offering. Once the bookmaker has received these prices, the early morning prices can no longer be taken. The board prices will change continually as money is bet on the runners up to the start of the race. Each new set of prices that is transmitted is called a show. The first set of prices transmitted is called the first show. The name board prices comes from the old custom of writing the prices on a board in a betting shop. As the start of the race approaches, the prices change with greater frequency.

Starting prices

Usually abbreviated to SP, the starting prices are an average of the prices that a sample of on-course bookmakers are offering at the start of the race, as agreed by the starting price executive. The starting price executive is made up of three major media companies, the Press Association, Trinity Mirror and Satellite Information Services. They employ starting price returners who make a note of prices offered in the betting ring for all the horses in each race, just before the off. An average of these prices is used to calculate the starting price.

When the results of the races are published in the press, the starting prices will be quoted. If you have taken a price like an early price or ante-post price, then your bet will be settled as the odds taken, regardless of the starting price. If you do not take any of the prices previously mentioned, then your bet will be settled at the starting price. In the event that no prices are quoted, the bets will be settled using the tote dividends.

Tote dividends

Tote dividends are quoted by the official tote on the racecourse. In the UK, it is possible to bet on the tote via ToteSports. For bets at tote odds, there are dividends quoted to a £1 stake for win, place, forecast, tricast, placepots and jackpots.

The dividends returned can vary quite considerably from the starting prices. This tends to happen more frequently at minor race meetings where the betting market is not strong.

Forecast and tricast

These are quoted to a £1 stake from the racecourse. Sometimes bookmakers may offer their own forecast prices, most commonly for foreign racing, where a dividend may not be given from the racecourse.

Betting on foreign racing

Depending on where you live you may or may not be able to bet on foreign racing. In the UK, it is possible to bet on racing all over the world. In the United States, you are restricted to betting in only in the state in which you live (if online betting is legal there). With the innovation of satellite transmission of racing, it is becoming more common for coverage to be given for major foreign racing. Simulcasting allows bettors in another country to bet directly into the pools at a foreign racecourse. An example of this is betting on the Breeders' Cup and the Prix de l'Arc de Triomphe, which allow British bettors to bet on the tote at the racecourse.

If you bet with British bookmakers on French racing you may have the choice of betting on the pari-mutuel (French tote) or with the bookmakers' prices. It is not possible to predict which is better, but at least if you take a price you know in advance what your winnings will be.

Pari-mutuel dividends

Pari-mutuel is the name of the French horseracing tote. The dividends are quoted to a one Euro stake.

One major difference with the French system of betting is the coupling of horses. If horses from the same stable are running in the same race, then the same price for those horses will be given in the betting. The horses are said to be coupled. A bet on one horse from that stable is also a bet on any one of the other horses from the same stable. Therefore, if horses A and B are coupled and a £1 win is placed on horse A, the bet will also win if horse B wins.

If, however, you take the bookmaker's price on a horse, your horses will not be coupled.

Types of bet

Bookmakers offer a wide variety of bets. Some of the most common are as follows.

Win single

This is one bet on the winner of a race.

Each way single

Two bets, one bet for the selection to win and the other for it to be placed. The place bet is settled as a fraction of the win odds. The number of places and the fraction of odds vary depending on how many runners there are and the type of race as shown in Table 5.2.

Number of runners	Type of race	Number of places	Fraction of win odds
16 or more	handicap	4	1/4
12 to 15	handicap	3	1/4
8 to 15	not applicable	3	1/5
5 to 7	not applicable	2	1/4
4 or less	not applicable	1 (win only)	both bets win

table 5.2 number of places and fraction of odds paid for the place bet, determined by number of runners and type of race

Double

A win double is one bet on two runners to win two different races. If the first selection wins, the returns are put onto the second selection.

An each-way double is two separate bets of a win double and a place double on two runners in two different races. The win bet is the same as a win double. For the place part of the bet, if the first selection is placed the returns become the stake for the second selection to be placed.

Treble

This is one bet on three selections in three different races. If the first selection wins, the returns are put on to the second selection and if the second selection wins the returns are put onto the third selection.

Accumulator

A bet on any number of selections, in different races, where the winnings on the first horse go onto the second and then onto the third and then onto the fourth and so on. It is one bet win and two bets each way. Obviously, the returns can be quite large, depending on the prices of the winning selections. It is therefore worth checking that your winnings would not exceed the bookmaker's maximum payout.

Straight forecast

Nominating which selections will finish first and second in the correct order.

Reversed forecast

Nominating two selections to finish first and second in either order. It is two bets.

Combination/full cover forecast

Selecting any number of runners in one race to finish first and second in either order. To calculate how may bets there are, simply multiply the number of selections by one number fewer.

For example:
  three selections is 3 × 2 = six bets
  four selections is 4 × 3 = 12 bets
  five selections is 5 × 4 = 20 bets.

Tricast

Selecting three runners in the same race to finish first, second and third in the correct order.

Trixie

Three selections in three different races, comprising three doubles and one treble. It is four bets win and eight bets each way.

Yankee

Four selections in four different races, comprising six doubles, four trebles and one fourfold. It is 11 bets win and 22 bets each way.

Super yankee/Canadian

Five selections in five different races, comprising 10 doubles, 10 trebles, five fourfolds and one fivefold. It is 26 bets win and 52 bets each way.

Heinz

Six selections in six different races comprising 15 doubles, 20 trebles, 15 fourfolds, six fivefolds and one sixfold. It is 57 bets win and 114 bets each way.

Super heinz

Seven selections in seven different races, comprising 21 doubles, 35 trebles, 35 fourfolds, 21 fivefolds, seven sixfolds and one sevenfold. It is 120 bets win and 240 bets each way.

Goliath

Eight selections in eight different races, comprising 28 doubles, 56 trebles, 70 fourfolds, 56 fivefolds, 28 sixfolds, eight seven folds and one eightfold. It is 247 bets win and 494 bets each way.

Patent/twist

Three selections in three different races, comprising three singles, three doubles and one treble. There are seven bets win and 14 bets each way.

Lucky 15

Four selections in four different races, comprising four singles, six doubles, four trebles and one fourfold. It is 15 bets win and 30 bets each way. If there are four winners, a 10 per cent bonus is paid, usually at starting price. If there is only one winner, double the starting price odds are paid. These bonuses and consolations apply only to the win part of the bet. So if an each-way lucky 15 has just one placed horse, double the odds is not paid on the placed selection. Similarly, if one selection wins and one is a non-runner, the consolation is not paid.

Lucky 31

Five selections in five different races, comprising five singles, 10 doubles, 10 trebles, five fourfolds and one fivefold. It is 31 bets win and 62 bets each way.

The bonuses paid vary with different bookmakers. Some pay a bonus on four winners and five winners, others pay a bonus on only five winners. It is certainly worth shopping around to find the best offers. A consolation of double the starting price odds is paid for one winner.

Lucky 63

Six selections in six different races, comprising six singles, 15 doubles, 20 trebles, 15 fourfolds, six fivefolds and one sixfold. It is 63 bets win and 126 bets each way.

Bonuses vary with different bookmakers. A 10 per cent bonus is usually paid for five winners. For six winners, the bonus is likely to be between 15 and 25 per cent. A consolation of double starting price odds is paid for one winner.

Betting Exchanges

What is a betting exchange?

Betting exchanges were introduced in 2000. Initially, concerns were raised about their affecting the integrity of racing due to them allowing bets on losing horses. These concerns have now been addressed with safeguards in place to monitor irregular patterns of betting. Due to the competitive prices offered, they have now become a popular way of betting.

A betting exchange acts as an agent to allow individuals to place bets with one another, charging a commission for its services. Suppose you wanted to have a bet with your friend on the favourite on the first race at Ascot. You think the horse will win and your friend thinks the horse will lose. You agree to each stake £50 and whoever wins takes the money staked. If your horse wins, you win the £100 and if your horse loses your friend wins the £100. In this situation, you have made a bet at 'evens' that your horse will win and your friend has made a bet at 'evens' that the horse will lose.

A betting exchange makes it possible for you to make bets like this except with strangers. They provide the facilities to make the betting possible and charge a commission for their services. They provide a website that allows you to come into contact with other people who want to bet and the means to transfer money from one person to another. Both you and the other bettors remain anonymous to each other. The betting exchange will keep details of the bets you have placed so that any foul play, such as people trying to manipulate the markets, can be investigated.

Unlike a bookmaker, the betting exchange does not decide the prices of the horses, instead the individuals making bets do. In the example just given, each person had agreed to odds of evens. However, they could have decided to bet at different odds. Suppose your friend wanted to bet but was only willing to stake £25 and you were willing to bet £50. You would then be betting at odds of 1/2 that your horse would win and your friend would be betting at odds of 2/1 that the horse would lose. If the horse wins you will win £75 less commission. If the horse loses your friend will win £75 less commission. If you were placing the bet with a betting exchange you would basically indicate that you wanted to make a bet of 1/2 on the horse and therefore needed someone to make the opposite bet of 2/1. As soon as someone agrees to match your bet, it is made.

This arrangement gives greater flexibility than betting with a bookmaker. With a bookmaker, you can only bet on horses to win. With a betting exchange you can also bet that a horse will lose. With a traditional bookmaker, a horse may have a price of, for example, 4/1 and you can bet that the horse will win at 4/1. The bookmaker is effectively backing the horse to lose at 1/4. With a betting exchange, you also have the opportunity to take the place of the bookmaker and bet that the horse will lose at 1/4.

Minimum stakes vary but are around £1 to £2. Unlike with a bookmaker there is no maximum bet. As long as you can find someone to match your bet, you can stake as much as you wish.

Commission is charged at around 1 to 5 per cent. Different exchanges calculate the commission in different ways. Some charge commission on all bets placed (stakes) and others charge commission on net winnings. Some exchanges reduce the commission for loyal customers so that the more you bet the less the commission charged. Currently bets are tax free, however this may change in the future as governments introduce new legislation.

Advantages of using a betting exchange

The prices with a betting exchange are around 17 to 20 per cent better than those offered by bookmakers. This is because bookmakers factor in a profit on every book that they make in order to cover their overheads and to make a profit. Since you are betting against an individual on a betting exchange, this does not apply. The prices will be determined by what other people are prepared to risk. Since they are only backing one horse, they do not have to make profit on all horses running, as a bookmaker has to. You also have the advantage that you can ask for a better price than is currently on offer and wait for someone to match your request.

There is a huge amount of competition for customers, which means tax-free betting, low commission rates, initial free bets and bonuses are all offered.

A betting exchange also offers more betting opportunities like betting on a photo finish.

The bets can be placed in the privacy of your own home.

You are not punished for winning. With a traditional bookmaker, you are likely to get barred or have your bets limited if you consistently win. However, with a betting exchange you are not playing against the exchange but against other individuals so the exchange does not lose out if you win. They make their money from commission on your bets so the more you bet, the better it is for the exchange.

There is no limit to the size of your bets. As long as you can find a match, you can bet to the level of stakes that your capital allows.

As prices change, you also have the opportunity to hedge bets and lock in a profit.

Disadvantages of using a betting exchange

Big bets cannot always be placed. Bets are limited to the stakes of the players betting. A traditional bookmaker is able to take most high-stake bets but with a betting exchange you are limited by what the other players want to bet.

You can't bet with cash, you need to deposit money with the exchange or use a bank or credit card.

You need to have a computer and internet connection.

Care also needs to be taken to avoid scams, fraud and identity theft.

Types of bet

You can bet on horses to win, lose, place or not place. It is also possible to bet on the winning distance of a horse. Betting on a horse to win is called backing and betting on a horse to lose is called laying. There are two main markets that you can bet on. The win market and the place market. The win market is for horses to win or lose. The place market is for horses to be placed or unplaced.

A place bet is just one bet for the horse to finish in the first two, three or four places depending on how many runners there are. The number of places will depend on how many horses are running and on the firm's rules. As a general guide the number of places paid is usually as follows:

5–7 runners, first and second
8–15 runners, first, second and third
16+ runners (non-handicap), first, second and third
16+ runners (handicap), first, second, third and fourth.

A bet on a horse being placed is not the same as each way (which is two bets and includes a bet for the horse to win and for it to place). If you want to make an each-way bet with a betting exchange you will need to make two bets – one on the win market and one on the place market.

Decimal odds

Like the tote at race courses, the odds are displayed as decimals, with the stake included in the price so, for example, 4/1 is 5, evens is 2 and 13/8 is 2.63. The decimals are shown to two places. Table 5.3 shows traditional odds converted to decimal odds.

Converting traditional odds to decimal odds

To convert a traditional price to decimal odds, you add both sides of the price then divide by the number on the right. For example, to convert 4/1 to a decimal:

$4 + 1 = 5$

$5 \div 1 = 5$

To convert 13/8 to a decimal:

$13 + 8 = 21$

$21 \div 8 = 2.625$, which is rounded up to 2.63

Converting decimal odds to traditional odds

To find the traditional odds to one stake unit, deduct one from the decimal odds. This then gives you the number on the left of the price to one.

For example decimal odds of 4.0 are traditional odds of 3/1. Decimal odds of 7.5 are $7.5 - 1 = 6\frac{1}{2}$ to 1, which is traditionally shown as 13/2.

Traditional odds	Decimal odds	Traditional odds	Decimal odds
100/1	101	85/40	3.13
66/1	67	2/1	3
50/1	51	15/8	2.88
40/1	41	7/4	2.75
33/1	34	13/8	2.63
25/1	26	6/4	2.5
20/1	21	7/5	2.4
18/1	19	11/8	2.38
16/1	17	5/4	2.25
15/1	16	6/5	2.2
14/1	15	11/10	2.1
12/1	13	21/20	2.05
13/1	14	1/1 evens	2
11/1	12	20/21	1.9
10/1	11	10/11	1.91
9/1	10	5/6	1.83
17/2	9.5	4/5	1.8
8/1	9	8/11	1.73
15/2	8.5	4/6	1.67
7/1	8	8/13	1.62
13/2	7.5	4/7	1.57
6/1	7	8/15	1.53
11/2	6.5	1/2	1.5
5/1	6	40/85	1.47
9/2	5.5	4/9	1.45
4/1	5	2/5	1.4
7/2	4.5	4/11	1.36
100/30	4.33	1/3	1.33
3/1	4	3/10	1.3
11/4	3.75	2/7	1.29
5/2	3.5	1/4	1.25
12/5	3.4	2/9	1.22
9/4	3.25	1/5	1.2

table 5.3 traditional odds to decimal odds

How the odds are shown

The odds are presented in a different way from bookmakers' odds. As different people offer different odds there will be several prices shown for each horse. The odds are presented in the form of a table and displayed from a backer's point of view. The table shows the value of bets that are currently unmatched for a particular price. There are odds displayed for the horses to win and to lose. The odds section of the table is divided into two halves – one half for back odds and the other half for lay odds. The back odds, for the horse to win, are typically listed on the left of the table and the lay odds for the horse to lose are on the right. The odds available are arranged in columns. The best odds are usually shown in a coloured or highlighted column.

An example of a betting screen for a betting exchange is shown in Table 5.4. The table is headed with the time and place of the race and is divided into two halves. The left side shows the back odds and the right side shows the lay odds. Next to the horses name are several different prices accompanied by an amount. These prices and amounts are arranged in columns. The best current odds are displayed in the column adjacent to the horse's name and are highlighted. In this case, the closer the column is to the outside of the table, the worse the odds. The amount underneath each price is the current maximum that can be bet at those odds. It represents unmatched bets. The amount is the total of all the bets offered at that price. It can be the stakes from more than one person. For example, the 9.8 £54 could be one bet for £50 and one bet for £4.

The prices in the back section are the prices at which you can back a horses to win. The amount underneath is how much can currently be bet at that price. Once that amount has been reached, the figure to the left will take its place.

		Back	**14:30 Ascot**	**Lay**		
4.1	4.2	4.3	Lucky Chance	4.4	4.5	4.6
£2191	£1692	£1558		£1931	£1050	£1249
9.8	10	10.5	Dobbin	11	11.5	13.5
£54	£497	£2		£266	£200	£8
17.5	18	18.5	Fast Filly	19.5	21	22
£43	£35	£249		£10	£20	£2
15.5	16.5	17	Slow Coach	21	22	23
£155	£121	£8		£2	£66	£6

table 5.4 how odds are presented

Back odds

In this example, the best price available for Dobbin to win is 10.5, the £2 underneath the 10.5 is the amount of unmatched stakes at that price. This means that someone is willing to offer odds of 10.5 for a stake of £2. The next best odds are 10 and it possible to bet up to £497 at this price. After this the next best odds are 9.8 with up to £54 being available to bet. From a backer's point of view, the highest number is the best price. It represents the multiple of the stake that will be won by the backer if the horse wins.

To back £2 at odds of 10.5, you would click on the price. You will then be taken to a betting screen (the equivalent of a betting slip). The odds of 10.5 will be displayed and there will be a box for you to enter your stake. You enter £2. Your profit (£19) will be displayed. You will then need to confirm the bet in order to place it. On the screen displaying the odds, the price of 10.5 will then disappear and will be replaced by the next best odds of 10 £497. If you decided to bet a further £2 at odds of 10 after making your bet 10 £495 would now be displayed in the best odds column.

Suppose you want to stake £10 on Dobbin to win and wanted to take the best price on offer you would then bet £2 at odds of 10.5 and £8 at odds of 10.

Lay odds

When you lay a bet, you are acting like a traditional bookmaker. If the backer wins (the horse wins), you payout his winnings but if the backer loses (the horse loses) you win his stake.

Suppose there is 6.0 and £10 on the lay side. If you decide to lay at these odds, you will win £10 if the horse loses. However, like a bookmaker, if the horse wins, you will lose £50.

If you look at the bet in terms of traditional odds, 6 is odds of 5/1. As you are laying the bet, you are taking the place of the bookmaker, you are making the bet of 1/5. In terms of money, you lay £50 and the backer stakes £10. The bet from your point of view is £10/£50. You stand to win £10 but in order to win you must stake £50. If you win (i.e. the horse loses) you will get the backer's stake of £10 and keep your stake of £50. If you lose (i.e. the horse wins), the backer will get your £50 stake and will keep his stake of £10.

In Table 5.5, the best price available for Dobbin to lose is 11, the £266 underneath the price is the amount of £266 of unmatched bets at a price of 11. The £266 represents bets that have been placed by backers that are currently unmatched. The next best odds are 11.5 and the maximum amount of money that is unmatched is £200. After this the next best odds are 13.5 with £8 being available to bet. From a layer's point of view, the lowest number is the best price. It represents the multiple of the backer's stake that will be lost by the layer if the horse wins. For example, by laying £266 at odds of 11, a layer will win £266 less commission if the horse loses. In order to win this he needs to stake £2660. If the horse wins the layer will lose his £2660 stake, which will be paid to the backers.

How bets are matched

A bet is not actually made until it is matched. If someone backs a horse £100 at 5.00 and someone is willing to lay those odds then the bet is matched. A bet may be matched by one or more people. For example, someone may match £60 worth of the bet and another person £40. Once bets are matched they cannot be cancelled.

The bets are held in a queue and are dealt with in the order in which they arrive at the site's server. The queue works on a first-come first-served basis, so it pays to place bets early in order to get a match. Any bets that are not matched by the start of the race will be void and the stakes refunded. The better the odds that you offer, the more likely you are to get a match.

Partial matching

Suppose you want to stake £10 on Dobbin at odds of 10.5. On the betting screen, you would enter odds of 10.5 and your stake of £10. £2 of your bet would be matched and the remaining £8 would be unmatched. On the lay side of the odds, 10.5 £8 would appear, with the current best price of 11 £266 moving one place to the right. Once your 10.5 £8 stake has been matched it will disappear from the odds screen.

The odds for Dobbin are now as shown in Table 5.5.

9.8	10	Dobbin	10.5	11	11.5
£54	£497		£8	£266	£200

table 5.5 odds for Dobbin

If someone decides to lay these odds, that is bet £8 at 10, your bet would be matched and the betting screen will now be as shown in Table 5.6.

9.8	10	Dobbin	11	11.5	13.5
£54	£497		£266	£200	£8

table 5.6 your bet is matched

On your personal account screen it would show that your £10 bet at odds of 10.5 has been matched. Now that your bet has been matched it can no longer be cancelled.

Ordering odds

If the odds that you want are not currently available you can place an order for them. Your bet may be fully matched, partially matched or unmatched. If your order is matched then the bet is made. If your order is not matched by the time of the off then your bet is void. There is a limit to the odds than can be ordered. Odds lower than 1.01 are not allowed odds over 1000 not allowed.

If, for example, odds of 4.5 are offered for a horse to win and you want odds of at least 5.0 and want to stake £100, then you place an order for odds of 5.0 and offer a stake of £100. If another person is willing to lay at these odds, that is bet that the horse will lose, then your bet is matched. Your bet can be matched up to your maximum stake of £100. Your bet will be made if someone is prepared to stake £500 that the horse will lose. That is enough to pay out your winnings. What may happen is that your bet is matched with several people's lay bets. For example, one lay bet of £10, one lay bet of £20 and one lay bet of £50. If by the off these are the only three matches then you will have a bet of £80 at odds of 5.0. The additional £20 will be void. If the horse wins, you will receive £420, where £400 is your winnings and £20 is void. Commission will be calculated on the net winnings of £320. At 5 per cent, the commission will be £16. You will therefore receive £404.

If you offer odds to other betters you will need to make your odds competitive in order to get a match.

To stop ridiculous odds being offered like 1000/1 when the current odds are 5/1, an order can usually only be placed within a certain increment of the current best price. You will need to consult the exchange rules for the increments.

Example

You could bet £2 at odds of 10.5 and place an order for £8 at odds of 10.5. Your £8 bet would only be valid if someone else is willing to match it.

9.8	10	10.5	Dobbin	11	11.5	13.5
£54	£497	£2		£266	£200	£8

table 5.7 original screen

If you took this option, the 10.5 odds would disappear from the highlighted column to be replaced by the odds of 10. On the lay side, your odds of 10.5 with £8 underneath would appear in the highlighted column where it will remain until someone matches it, that is, decides they want to stake £8 at a price of 10.5 that the horse will lose.

9.8	10	Dobbin	10.5	11	11.5
£54	£497		£8	£266	£200

table 5.8 after placing your order

Best odds

If you place a bet at the odds of 6.0 and odds of 6.5 are available then your bet will be matched at these odds as they are better than 6.0. They will not be matched with odds of 5.5 as these are worse odds.

Back all and lay all

The betting screen also gives you the opportunity to back all the runners. This is backing the entire field to win, that is all horses that are running.

Lay all is laying the entire field, that is all the horses to lose.

Official result

All winning bets are settled according to the official result at the time of the 'weigh-in'. This means that if, for example, a horse is later disqualified due to a positive drug test, the result at the 'weigh-in' still counts.

Non-runners

If a horse is a non-runner, all unmatched and matched bets on the horse are void. If the race is a walkover (there is only one runner) all bets are void on that race. If a horse is withdrawn from a race once a market has been formed then depending on the price of the withdrawn horse, the prices on the remaining horses may be lowered. You are advised to check the betting exchange's rules.

The amount that the price is reduced by is a percentage and called the reduction factor. It is based on the rule 4 system that bookmakers use. Prior to betting on a race, each horse is given a reduction factor based on the exchange's estimates of each horse's chance of winning. Unmatched bets to lay will be cancelled.

In the win market, reductions are made on the whole odds. With a matched bet at odds of 6.00 and a horse with a reduction factor of 20 per cent, your odds will be reduced by 20 per cent and become odds of 4.80.

In a place market, the reduction factor is made to the win portion of the odds. With a reduction factor of 25 per cent, the win portion of the odds will be reduced 25 per cent, odds of 8 would become 6.25.

Example

For a price of 8, the win portion is the price minus the stake

8 − 1 = 7

7 × 25% = 1.75

8 − 1.75 = 6.25

Dead heat

In the event of a dead heat, the odds are divided by the number of declared winners for the market. Suppose two horses dead heat for first place and you have backed one of the winners at a price of 5. You will be paid out at a price of 2.5.

How to bet

From the site's home page, you need to go to the race that you want to bet on. This will take you to the betting screen with the prices. The odds will be constantly changing as more money is bet on a race. Near the off of a race, the situation can quickly change. With some sites, the screen will automatically change to show the new odds but with some you may need to refresh the screen to see the most up to date odds.

Betting options

You have several options:

- to back a horse at the current odds available
- to lay a horse at the current odds available
- to place an order for back odds of your choice
- to place an order for lay odds of your choice
- to back all
- to lay all
- to cancel unmatched bets.

Back a horse at current odds

Suppose you want to bet £100 on a horse to win at odds of 2.0 and these odds are available, you place your bet by clicking on the box containing these odds. You will be taken to a screen that is the equivalent of a betting slip. This screen will show the odds and will prompt you to enter your stake. You will then be taken to another screen to confirm your bet.

You have the option of cancelling your bet as long as it is not matched. If just a portion of your bet has been matched, you also have the option of cancelling the unmatched portion. Once a bet has been fully matched it can no longer be cancelled. If the horse wins, you will win £200 less commission. If the horse loses, you will lose £100.

Lay a horse at current odds

Suppose you want to lay £100 on a horse to lose. Lay odds of 2.5 are offered and there is £500 unmatched. In order to place a bet, you place click on the box containing these odds. You will be taken to a screen that is the equivalent of a betting slip. This screen will show the odds and will prompt you to enter the stake. You need to enter the backer's stake that you are willing to match. You enter £100. Your liability is £150 and will be displayed on the screen. The liability of £150 is how much you will lose if the horse wins. The stake of £100 will be how much you will win from the backer if the horse loses.

Calculating your liability

To calculate your liability you need to deduct one from the decimal price and multiply the remainder by the backer's stake. In the last example, the decimal price is 2.5. The backer's stake is £100:

2.5 − 1 = 1.5
1.5 × 100 = 150
liability = £150

Calculating commission

The betting exchange charges commission for its services. Commission is typically paid on net winnings at a rate of around 5 per cent. This compares favourably to a traditional bookmaker where a charge of around 10 to 20 per cent is made.

Example

You back £100 at 5 and win. Your returns are £500. Your stake is £100. Net profit is 500 − 100 = £400.

Commission = 400 x 5% = £20

Profit after commission = 400 − 20 = £380

Returns = 380 + 100 = £480

You lay £100 at 5 and win. Your returns are £100. Your stake is £400. Your returns are £500. Net profit is 500 − 400 = £100.

Commission = 100 x 5% = £5

Profit after commission = 100 − 5 = £95

Returns = 95 + 400 = £495

Book percentage

The book percentage or over-round tells you how profitable a book is. The book percentage is shown for the back and lay markets. It shows how competitive the prices on offer are. It is calculated by adding the individual percentage chance of each selection based on the price that it being offered. A book that is perfectly balanced will have a percentage of 100 per cent. In this case, both backers and layers would break even. If you are laying all selections in a market (like a traditional bookmaker) you should ensure your book percentage is greater than 100 per cent, then you are guaranteed to make a profit. If the book percentage is lower than 100 per cent you will lose money.

If you place bets with a book percentage greater than 100 per cent, and all your bets are matched, you will make money.

If you are backing a selection, you would ideally look for a market where the book percentage was as low as possible, that is as close as possible to 100 per cent. Occasionally a book percentage will go lower than 100 per cent (overbroke). In theory, you could then back every selection and guarantee a profit.

Spread betting

What is spread betting?

Spread betting started about 25 years ago and was used as a way to speculate on the financial markets. Bets were placed on how much the stock exchange would go up or down on a certain day. This form of gambling has been adapted for betting on horse racing.

Instead of betting on individual horses winning or losing, it is betting on combinations of events like how the favourites will perform at a meeting, what the starting prices of all the winning horses will be and what the winning distances will be. The spread betting company will make a prediction about a particular event. You need to decide if their prediction is too high or too low. The more you're right, the more you win and the more you're wrong, the more you lose. Due to its connection with the financial markets, the terms buying and selling are used. Buying is betting higher and selling is betting lower.

It has a higher level of financial risk than traditional betting. With traditional betting you know beforehand how much you will lose if your bet loses. You simply lose the amount you stake. With spread betting it is possible to have huge losses. To restrict the amount you can lose, it is possible to place a stop order on a bet.

Spread betting on favourites

A spread betting company will give a favourites' index at each meeting. This index is based on a score given to favourites that are placed in a race. The scores given can vary but as a general guide a favourite is awarded 25 points for winning, 10 points for coming second, five points for third place and 0 points for finishing in any other position. If there are joint favourites, then the one with the lowest race card number is considered the favourite.

To place a bet, you need to decide whether to bet higher or lower than the predicted score. If, for example, the predicted score is 70 and you think the likely score is higher then you bet high (buy). If you think the predicted score will be lower then you bet low.

The payout is calculated on the basis of how much higher or lower the score is.

If you bet £2 high and the result is 85 then you win 15 times your stake: $(85 - 70) \times$ your stake $= 10 \times £2 = £30$.

If you bet low and the result is 80 then you lose 10 times your stake: $(80 - 70) \times$ your stake $= 10 \times £2 = -£20$.

Jockey performance index

This is a bet on how a jockey performs in a meeting. A jockey is awarded 25 points for winning a race, 10 points for coming second, five points for coming third and no points for any other position. The spread betting firm will quote an index for each jockey at the meeting. You need to decide if the result will be higher or lower than the predicted index.

At a race meeting a jockey is predicted as having a performance of 32–34 points. You can bet higher than 34 or lower than 32.

Suppose you bet £10 lower. If the jockey's score is 25, you win £70: $(32 - 25) \times 10 = £70$. If the jockey's score is 80, you will lose £460: $(80 - 34) \times 10 = £460$.

Starting prices (SPs) of the winners

This is a bet on the total of the starting prices of all the winners at a race meeting. A 4/1 winner is four points, 10/1 is 10 points up to a maximum of 50/1 or 50 points so a 100/1 winner will have 50 points.

The SP prediction may be 55–58. If you predict that the result will be higher, you bet high, if you think it will be lower then you bet low.

Match bets

This is a bet on the distance between two nominated horses in a race. The maximum makeup on for flat races is 12 lengths and 15 lengths for national hunt. A short head is 0.1 of a length, a head is 0.2 and a neck 0.3, half a length 0.5, three-quarters of a length 0.75.

Race index

This is a bet on an individual horse. Bets are placed on whether or not a horse's index will be higher or lower than the prediction.

Example

The number of points awarded will depend on how many runners there are in a race.

For races with over 12 runners:
50 points for first
30 points for second
20 points for third
10 points for fourth
0 points for any other position

Races with up to 12 runners:
50 points for first
25 points for second
10 points for third

A horse is predicted to get 13–16 points. You bet £1 higher at 16. Maximum win is £34; maximum risk is £16.

The horse finishes sixth so has no points. The difference between the price and the result is 16 − 0 = 16. Loss = £1 x 16 = £16.

Double race card numbers

This is a bet based on the total of the winners' doubled race card number at a meeting. For example, if the race card number of the winners of a meeting were numbers 2, 5, 11, 7, 3 and 6, this totals 34. The result would be 2 x 34 = 68.

If the prediction had been 75–79 and you had bet £10 low (sell), the difference between the result and the prediction is 75 − 68 = 7. Your winnings would be £10 × 7 = £70.

Heavyweights index

Here the performance of the heavyweights is predicted.

Winning distances

Here the total winning margins for a meeting is predicted.

Leave yourself time

When betting over the internet, make sure you leave enough time for a bet to be processed. With the internet you need to take account of traffic and the time delay for processing information from one computer to another. Although your computer may show that you placed a bet before the off time of a race, due to the time it takes for the information to leave your computer, reach your internet service provider and then to reach the bookmaker's internet service provider and then the bookmaker's computer, your bet may be too late. The time the bet left your computer is not what counts, it is the time at which the bookmaker's computer received your bet.

This time delay may also mean that you miss out on the odds that you want. Odds can rapidly change, especially before the off of a race and you need to be quick to place your bet at the desired odds. If you are not fast enough to place your bet, you will miss some odds.

Getting started with a betting exchange

If using a betting exchange is new to you, start out with small stakes until you get used to the concept. Don't forget that lay bets are the opposite proposition to back bets. With back bets you lose just your stake if your horse loses but with lay bets you pay out the winnings if the horse wins. Take particular care with laying bets as you can easily lose high multiples of stakes, particularly if you start laying all the horses in a race. Although you are acting like a bookmaker, you haven't got the bookmakers 17 per cent guaranteed profit built into the prices. Online bookmakers do go bust leaving the bettors unpaid so keep only the minimum that you need to bet in the internet account and clear out any winnings as soon as possible. If your exchange does go bust, then your losses will be minimized.

Hedging

Hedging a bet is making an additional bet to guarantee a profit. Because a betting exchange allows you back and lay, you are able to take advantage of price changes and ensure you make a profit regardless of the outcome of the race. Suppose you have bet on a horse to win £100 at 20.0 and its price drops down to 8.0. If you then lay £250 at 8.0, you will make a profit of £150 (less commission) regardless of whether the horse wins or loses.

If the horse wins, your back bet, £100 at 20.0, wins, giving a return of £2000. The stake is £100 so the profit is £1900. Your lay bet £250 at 8.0 loses and you lose £1750.

Your net profit on the two bets is 1900 –1750 = £150.

If the horse loses, your lay bet £250 at 800 wins, giving a return of £250. Your back bet, £100 at 20.0 loses, so you lose your stake of £100. Your net profit on the two bets is £250 – £100 = £150.

You could also hedge just a portion of your bet, for example, you initially back £100 at 20.0, the price drops and you lay just £100 at 8.0. If the horse wins, your win bet £100 at 20 wins, giving a return of £2000. The stake is £100 so the profit is £1900. Your lay bet £100 at 8.0 loses and you lose £700. Your net profit on the two bets is 1900 – 700 = £1200.

If the horse loses, your win bet £100 at 20.0 loses and you lose your stake of £100. Your lay bet, £100 at 8.0, wins and you win £100. Your net profit on the two bets is zero.

In this situation, you win £1200 if the horse wins and you lose nothing if it loses.

Time lags

It is possible to take advantage of time lags as it takes time for the prices from the race course to have an effect on the exchange prices. One of the best times to take advantage of price changes is while other races are running. On a Saturday, for example, there may be a race off at 3.30 and another at 3.35, while the 3.30 race is running, most people who have bet on the earlier race will be watching it, and will not be concentrating on what is happening to the prices on the 3.35 race. By comparing bookmakers' prices to exchange prices, there may be an opportunity to anticipate price moves and to make your bets while most of the other bettors are otherwise occupied.

There are sites on the internet that provide odds comparison services, they show you the prices across a range of bookmakers and exchanges allowing you to spot the firm offering the best price.

Sports betting

It is possible to bet on almost any sport on the internet via bookmakers, betting exchanges and spread betting firms. The basic principles of betting are similar to horse racing. Bookmakers offer sports betting at fixed odds. Betting exchanges allow the bettors to decide their own odds. Spread betting firms make predictions about sporting events and the customers bet on how correct those predictions are. Due to the value offered Asian handicaps and in-running betting on the exchanges are popular methods of betting on sports.

Asian handicaps

As the name suggests Asian handicaps originated in Asia. They were originally a way for friends to bet with one another on the outcome of a football match. With a football match, there are three possible outcomes – win, lose or draw. For most individuals, calculating three-way odds is complex. To simplify matters, each team was given odds of evens and a handicap to theoretically equalize their chance of winning. A team is given a half-, one-goal or more handicap. The handicap can be a positive or a negative figure. Where a fraction of a goal is used as a handicap, a draw is eliminated. The handicap is added to the final score to give the result on which the bet is settled. If, after taking the handicap into consideration, there is a draw, the stakes are refunded.

Example

Manchester Utd −0.5 odds = 2.1
Liverpool +0.5 odds = 1.9

If you bet on Liverpool to win, the handicap is added to Liverpool's final score. If the match is a draw at 1:1, taking into account the handicap, the result is Manchester 1, Liverpool 1.5. This means a win for Liverpool. Your bet wins and is paid at odds of 1.9. A £1 bet would return £1.90.

If you bet on Manchester Utd to win and the final score was 2:2, the handicap would be added to Manchester's score. The result would be Manchester Utd 1.5, Liverpool 2. Your bet would lose.

In some Asian handicap markets there may be two handicaps given for a team. In this case the stake is divided between the two handicaps.

> **Example**
>
> Manchester Utd 0 and –0.5 odds = 2.1
> Liverpool 0 and +0.5 odds = 1.9
>
> Final score Manchester 1, Liverpool 1
>
> £10 win Liverpool.
>
> £5 is placed on the handicap of 0 and £5 on the handicap of +0.5.
>
> For the handicap of zero the result is Manchester 1, Liverpool 1. This is a draw. The £5 stake is refunded.
>
> For the handicap of +0.5, the result is Manchester 1, Liverpool 1.5. Liverpool wins.
>
> The bet is settled at odds of 1.9. 1.9 x 5 = 6.9
>
> Total returns = 5 + 6.9 = £11.90

In-running betting

In-running betting is placing a bet on an event once it has started. For example, betting on the result of a football match after the kick-off. In-running betting can often provide value bets. For example, suppose you want to bet on the underdog in a football match, if you wait until the match has kicked off you can often get a better price than before. This is because the favourite will be highly backed and to balance their books, the bookmakers will lengthen the price on the other team.

06

selecting the winning horse

In this chapter you will learn:
- how to assess the runners
- where to find information about the runners
- about betting systems.

Deciding which horse to bet on in a race is not easy. Many factors influence the outcome of horse races. These include things like the jockey, the weight carried, the condition of the ground and the distance of the race. This makes betting on horse racing both interesting and challenging. A gambler needs to use his skill to assess the likely winner and or placed horses from a field of between two and up to 40 runners.

Even after taking into account all the different factors some aspects of horse racing are unpredictable. No matter how carefully you have assessed a horse's chances of winning, something can go wrong that will affect the outcome of a race. In national hunt races, horses can be brought down by others. Horses may slip on wet ground. The weights carried by the horse may be lost in the course of the race, causing the horse to be disqualified. Even the jockey's actions may result in a horse being disqualified. Races are run at a fast pace with the jockey making split-second decisions. His actions can result in other horses being impeded, which may lead to disqualification. In his eagerness to make a horse win, he may use his whip more frequently than is allowed under the rules.

A great deal of the information that you need to consider when assessing a horse's chance of winning is given by the race cards printed in newspapers and programmes. The format varies depending on the publication. To save space a lot of abbreviations are used. Take time to familiarize yourself with what all the abbreviations mean.

The analysis of all this information is very time consuming. In recent years computer programs have been developed to process this information. Using a computer can cut down on the work. There are many different programs on the market, all offering different features, so it is worth shopping around for the best deal.

There is now a wealth of information available on the internet. The amount of information is almost overwhelming. Lots of online racing magazines, horse racing websites and tipsters services now exist. Many provide up-to-date analysis of all the statistics like the performance of favourites, the influence of the draw, the top trainers, the top jockeys and pedigree information.

Factors you can assess

Pedigree

For all racehorses it is possible to trace back their pedigrees for hundreds of years. A good pedigree is an indication of a potentially good horse but not always. Horses are carefully bred to bring out characteristics that make good runners. Horses with good racing records are sent to stud in order to try to bring out those characteristics in future generations. However, due to the nature of genetics, the breeding of these characteristics is not always an exact science. A dam and sire with good racing records do not always produce fast offspring. Often the characteristics that make a good runner can skip generations.

One characteristic that has been shown to have a positive affect on the performance of horses is a large heart. Although this characteristic may be present in the sire it may not show up in his immediate offspring, only to reappear in later generations.

This can mean that a horse that may have had a poor racing record can sire fast offspring. This makes the study of pedigree an inexact method of finding winners. It tends to be used as a tool for finding winners where the horses have not run before.

Previous performance of the runners

Due to the unpredictability of breeding, a great deal of importance is placed on the previous performance of horses. Once the horse has actually run, you have a clearer indication of its potential. You will have information available about how the horses have performed in previous races. This is called form. Different racing publications publish this information in different formats. To cut down on space, abbreviations are used and each publication will give a key explaining them. As a general rule, the more detailed the information, the more you have to pay for it. You will therefore need to decide for yourself how important you feel the information is. The sorts of detail that are given are the results of previous races, the jockey, trainer, weight carried and a guide to the betting. When the horse has not run in many races in the current season, its performance for the previous season will be given.

Try to watch as many races as possible. The written data do not always show why a horse performed poorly. The jockey may have been at fault. He may have waited too long before pushing a horse. A horse may sprint quickly at the end of the race but if the jockey left it too late to push or was boxed in by other horses, it may still lose. A better jockey next time out may compensate.

Some horses may have an easy win, with the jockeys not having to use the whip or, alternatively, easing down near the finish. Other horses may win but under pressure from the jockey. A poorer jockey next time out may mean it loses. A horse could fall at a difficult fence. If the fences are easier in its next race, the horse may not be so unfortunate. A horse may lose a race over the jumps because it is brought down by a loose horse or slips on wet ground. With better running conditions, it may win its next race. With sprinting races, a horse may get off to a bad start. The next race may be better.

At the beginning of the season you will not have a lot of information on which to base your selection. As the season progresses, you will have a much better indication of how the horses are performing. Towards the end of the season, you will have many more consistent data on which to base your decisions. For this reason, you should bet cautiously at the beginning of the season and gradually increase stakes as the season progresses and you are more confident of your selections.

Speed of the horse

The speed that a horse can run is by far the clearest indication of how likely a horse is to win. No matter how good the jockey, the trainer or the condition of the ground, if a horse is not fast it is unlikely to win. Assessing the speed is not a simple matter. Factors like the amount of weight carried and the going all affect a horse's speed.

Timeform offer the most comprehensive records of the speed of horses. They produce a daily newspaper and separate books giving details of flat racing and national hunt statistics. For anyone seriously assessing a horse's chances of winning, this information is invaluable. (See taking it further, page 193.) You can, of course, accumulate the information yourself if you are prepared to commit the time it takes to gather data.

Harness racing

The United States Trotting Association keeps records of the fastest race a horse wins each year. Abbreviations are used to cut down on space. With harness racing, the comparison of the runners is made much easier as most races are run over a mile.

Example: p,3,Q1:58.1($100,000)

p – the horse gait p = pace, no letter = trot

3 – age of the horse, here it was a 3 year old

Q – the type of race. Q = qualifying race, T = time trial, no letter = during a race

1:58.1 – the time taken to run one mile, in this case one minute and 58⅕ seconds

the length of the track – f = ⅝ mile, s = ⅞ mile, h = ½ mile, no letter = 1 mile

($100,000) – the amount of money won by the horse in its career

---

The race

You don't have to bet on every race. Save your money for the races that offer the best prospects. It takes time to assess all the runners so concentrate on a few races each day. Certain races can be dismissed as it too difficult to predict the outcome. It is better to select races where you have a clear indication of a horse's performance. Avoid selling races, claiming races, maiden handicaps, apprentice races and amateur races. With the higher class races you will have a lot more information on which to base your decision. Clips of the horses' previous races run will be shown by the racing media and a lot more information will be written over these horses in horse racing publications.

Distance of the race

Most horses have an optimum distance over which they perform well. Some are excellent sprinters while others have stamina to cope with longer distances. If a horse is entered for a distance that it has never run before, its previous performance can provide some indication as to how well it will fare. Has the horse run shorter distances and won easily? Or has it run longer distances but lacked stamina and faded at the end? If you watch lots of racing you will notice these factors.

Change of class

The grade of race may have an effect on its outcome. If a horse performs particularly well in, for example, a Class 2 race, it may be entered for a Class 1 race. Since Class 1 races attract the best horses, it will be up against much stronger opposition than in its previous race. Avoid betting on horses that have moved up a class. Wait for them to prove themselves in their new class. It is also possible for horses to drop down a grade so a horse that has previously run in a Class 1 race may compete in a Class 2 race. The horse may have performed badly in the Class 1 race but the change of class may lead to a huge improvement. The form guides in newspapers give details of which horses are running in different classes.

Experience of the runners

Races in which the horses have never run before are notoriously difficult to pick the winners. The problem with betting on them is that you have no previous form on which to base your assessment. This is where the pedigree of the horse needs to be studied. You can glean the horse's potential by studying the racing records of its parents, the dam and sire. A much clearer indication can be achieved by going back several generations. They may also have produced other offspring that have already run that gives you more information on which to base your selection. The trainer, jockey and owner will also play a role in your selection.

A horse's experience can be particularly important over jumps. An inexperienced horse that has only recently been trained to jump is more likely to fall than one with more experience.

Flat races where the horses must start in stalls can cause problems. Experienced horses are more used to the stalls and less likely to be nervous. A nervous horse can easily injure itself and or the jockey in the stalls or simply refuse to race once it has been let out. You will also know of experienced horses that are nervous in the stalls.

Although an older horse has more experience, it may also be less fit than its rivals. You will need to decide at what stage the age of a horse becomes a negative factor. This is not always easy as some horses do have exceptional records even at an old age. Red Rum was 12 years old when he won his third Grand National. In 1980 Sonny Somers won two steeplechases at the age of 18.

The record for the oldest horse ever to win a race is held by Marksman, a horse that won a flat race at Ashford in 1826 aged 28 years old.

Condition of the ground ('the going')

The condition of the ground on the racecourse is called the going. Before the start of racing the clerk of the course will inspect the condition of the ground and declare the going. The going is classified from the fastest to the slowest conditions as follows:

• hard
• firm
• good to firm
• good
• good to soft
• soft/yielding
• heavy.

Since the courses do not drain evenly there may be patches of ground where the going differs from the rest of the course. For example, you may see the going quoted as 'good (good to firm patches)'. In order to get more consistent ground some tracks are watered. On all-weather tracks where the racing surface is made of fibre-sand, the going is fairly consistent and is quoted as standard.

The condition of the ground may affect how well a horse runs. For example, some run well on heavy ground, while others run poorly. You will have to ask yourself if the ground suits your selection. A horse may have won its last race on hard ground but if its next race is on heavy ground, you will need to assess what impact this change will have. By going back through the records you can see how well a horse performed on particular ground. If you attend a race meeting, you will be able to inspect the ground yourself and draw your own conclusions about how it will affect the horses.

A good time for betting can be towards the end of the flat season when the ground has usually dried out. This removes one of the unknown factors. Also by this stage the performance of the horses is known. This is traditionally a time of year when bookmakers start losing money.

Weather conditions

Always take note of the weather forecast. If it is expected to rain, bear in mind that the going may change. Ground that started out as good can easily become heavy after a huge downpour. Some horses fare better than others depending on weather conditions. Hot weather has a more adverse effect on bigger horses than it does on small ones.

The course

In the United States, the racetracks are of less importance, as they are mostly the same oval-shaped dirt tracks. In Great Britain, where the courses are all different, this can have an effect on how well a horse runs. Some courses have left-hand bends and others right. Some are flat. Others have slight inclines and some steep hills.

You will need to consider how the racecourse is going to affect a horse. The horse you select may have a preference for right-hand turns; therefore, you will need to assess the impact of a course with left-hand turns. A horse may run well on a flat course, but how is a hill going to affect his performance?

Starting stalls are used in flat racing to ensure that each horse starts at precisely the same time. The draw is the position in which the horse starts in the stalls – not to be confused with its race card number. At a lot of racecourses there are advantages to starting in certain positions in the stalls. The table on pages 109–11 details the effect of the draw.

Blinkers

Some horses are distracted by other horses and do not run well. Blinkers are an aid that allow a horse to see only in front of it; the other runners are excluded from its field of vision. If a horse is wearing blinkers for the first time, it is possible for there to be a marked improvement in its running.

Condition of the horse

In the course of racing and training horses may get injured. Nowadays, veterinary care is of the highest quality with excellent treatment available. The effect of an injury on a horse's future performance can be negligible. However, some horses may have recurrent injury problems that can make their performance unreliable. Keeping up to date with all the news will highlight any horses that are not entirely fit. Be wary of horses that are running after a long absence as they may have been injured or ill. They may have previously had good form but the impact of an injury or illness will need to be assessed.

Pregnancy (in foal) can be a big advantage to a horse. This is due to an increase in red blood cells, which allows more oxygen to be carried to the muscles and increases their efficiency, meaning a horse can run much faster.

The owner

The owner of a horse can also be included in your assessment. Some owners have particularly good reputations for spotting and buying good quality horses with the potential to win races. Your knowledge about owners can also help with the selection of horses on their first outings. If a particular owner has a good record of winners, a horse on its first outing entered in a race by him may have a better chance of winning than novices of other owners.

The trainer

All trainers are different. They employ a variety of methods for training horses – some are better than others. Some trainers also have good reputations for bring out the very best in a horse. You will need to keep up to date with the latest news to discover which trainers are producing winners. Another important factor is a change of trainer. A better trainer may improve the performance of a horse.

The jockey

Avoid unproven jockeys. Over shorter distances the jockey is less crucial. With longer distances, experienced jockeys will generally fare better as tactics play a part in the outcome. They will be better at pacing a race and keeping out of trouble. Stick to experienced jockeys over the jumps. An inexperienced jockey is more likely to fall off or pull up.

Keep up to date with jockey changes. A jockey may become ill or injured resulting in a horse having a different rider. The replacement may be better or worse so you will need to review your selection.

Number of runners

If you are making place or each-way bets keep up to date with the number of runners. A bet may not be worthwhile if you only get 1/5 odds instead of 1/4. A rule 4 deduction can also impact your bet.

Factors you cannot assess

Because horse racing is unpredictable, things can and do go wrong. All the studying in the world cannot guard against them.

Horses can have off-days too

Horses can be unpredictable. Even the most well-behaved horses can have off-days. If they don't want to cooperate with a jockey they will:

- dig their heels in and refuse to run
- not go into the starting stall
- refuse to jump fences
- attempt to throw the jockey.

You may know in advance that a horse has a reputation for being difficult, so it's best to avoid betting on it. Save your money for the runners you are certain of.

Other horses

It is common for horses to bring down others at jumps. A horse may be the best jumper in the world but if another horse gets in its way, it can easily fall. Loose horses can cause all sorts of problems. They can box in your selection, bump into it or run across its path, all of which can cause a horse to lose a race.

Weights

Weights can and do occasionally fall off in the course of a race. Jockeys also sometimes forget to weigh in after a race. Either of these situations results in disqualification.

False starts

A false start can ruin a horse's chance of winning – he may have run half of the race before being recalled. However, safeguards have been put in place to prevent a repeat performance of the 1993 British Grand National fiasco when several horses completed the course after a false start.

Other factors

Jockeys do occasionally take the wrong course. Horses can also escape from the jockey before the race. This can result in their being withdrawn from the race, particularly if they have used up a lot of energy running all over the course. Although you will have your stake refunded (unless, you've bet ante-post (see page 67)) if that horse is your selection, it can mean your hard work has been wasted, Alternatively, if your horse is still running, it can mean that adjustments to the betting make your bet unprofitable (if, for example, you have bet each way).

Although these incidents happen infrequently, you should bear them in mind as possibilities. It's tempting to stake a lot of money on a horse when you think it can't fail to win. By keeping your stakes to a reasonable level on each race, you will minimize your losses when these events do occur.

Gathering information

A lot of information is given by the race cards printed in newspapers or programmes. The format varies depending on the publication. To save space many abbreviations are used.

Example race card

2.00 Winner's Stakes £3,752 (4 run)

1(2) 2/1–132	Liberty Dawn (14) (B, CD)	J Jones 5 11 4	J Smith
2(3)	Bronze Cannon	F Evans 4 10 10	D Bolton
3(1) 111	Lucky Luc (28)	S Moon 4 10 10	S Heard
4(4)	Suzie's Boy	G Chip 5 11 4	K Bearman

Betting: 2 Lucky Luc, 4 Liberty Dawn, 10 Bronze Cannon, Suzie's Boy.

2.00	– time of the race
Winner's Stakes	– name of the race
£3752	– prize money to the winning owner
(4 run)	– number of runners
1	– race card number
(2)	– draw – position in starting stalls
01–132	– the horse's form in its last six races

1 = 1st, 2 = 2nd, 3 = 3rd, 0 = unplaced, d = disqualified

A dash (–) is a break of one season. An oblique (/) indicates two or more seasons' break. The figure on the right is the latest race. In national hunt racing the following abbreviations are also used: U = unseated rider; F = fell; B = brought down; P = pulled up; R = refused.

Liberty Dawn	– the name of the horse
(14)	– number of days since it last ran
(B, CD)	– meanings of abbreviations follow:

B = horse was wearing blinkers, headgear that restricts lateral vision

V = visor, blinkers that minimize awareness of activity on either side

H = a hood

E = eyeshield

B* = blinkers worn for the first time

BF = beaten favourite last time out

C = winner over the course

D = winner over the distance

CD	– course and distance winner
J Jones	– name of trainer
Betting	– rough guide to what the betting is likely to be
5 11 4	– a 5-year-old horse, carrying 11 stone 4
J Smith	– name of the jockey

Learn about horse racing

Become knowledgeable about horse racing. Read as many publications as possible. Ensure that you have a thorough understanding of the subject. Keep up to date with the latest news by reading a good-quality racing newspaper. (See taking it further on page 193 for details of racing publications.) The more information you have, the better able you are to assess a horse's chance of winning.

Keep your own records on the horses you are interested in. Use a diary to record events as they happen. You may notice something that others have missed.

Tipsters

Studying all these factors takes an enormous amount of time. If you lack the time to do it yourself there are other people who have already done all the hard work. They are the tipsters employed by the newspapers. They select the likely prospects that they think will win. There are also telephone and internet tipping services that charge for information.

However, you don't always know what system they're using to assess the horses and how good that system is. They may have missed an important factor that you may have noticed. The newspapers boast when their tipsters get it right but keep quiet when they don't – after all, they are in the business of selling newspapers. Over the course of the year tipsters are bound to get it wrong too.

Record predictors

The record for predicting the most winners in one day is held by Charles Lamb, racing correspondent for the *Baltimore News American*. In 1974 he picked out 10 winners at a meeting held at Delaware Park. Bob Butcher of the *Daily Mirror* correctly forecast seven winners for a meeting at Wolverhampton. So, too, did Fred Shawcross at a York meeting in 1988.

Systems

Looking through the small ads of publications will often turn up a number of advertisements for betting systems. There are lots of different systems and they often guarantee excellent returns.

Do they work? The sellers of such systems will tell you they do. Friends will boast that they have invented the ultimate system that never fails. Throughout the years many systems have been invented, some more successful than others.

Ignore all claims that are made about a system. To test how effective it is, try it out yourself on a dummy run. Don't bet any money. Make a note of results over a period of time and apply the system to those results. If it gives good returns, try it with small stakes. Continue to monitor results. If it starts failing, give up on it and try something else.

Developing your own systems for selecting horses

Try to develop your own systems for selecting horses to bet on. You will need to take account of all the influencing factors mentioned. Some are more important than others but all play a part. One method is to award points for each factor. Most importance should be place on the speed of a horse, with points added for factors that have a positive influence and points deducted for those that have a negative influence.

Doubling up on the favourite

Some systems involve no assessment of the runners. A popular system is doubling up on the favourite. Here, a bet is placed on the favourite in the first race. If that loses, the stake is doubled and placed on the favourite in the second race. This continues until there is a winner and the gambler stops betting.

This system falls down in several ways. The capital required to make it work can be huge. It may be some time before a favourite wins (they lose around 60 per cent of their races). If the favourite is a very low price (below 6/5) you will not recoup your outlay. There is always the danger that a horse could be withdrawn. This could bring the price of the favourite below the level that you need to break even. The potential rewards are also low.

Example

- First race £10 bet stake = £10.90. Total loss £10.90.
- Second race £20 bet stake = £21.80. Total loss £32.70.
- Third race £40 bet stake = £43.60. Total loss £76.30.
- Fourth race £80 bet stake = £87.20. Total loss £163.50.

In the fourth race the favourite wins at 1/2. Returns = £120.
Total loss = £43.50.
If the favourite had won at 2/1, returns = £240.
Total winnings = £76.50.

However, there is no guarantee that the favourite would win by the fourth race. If your stake becomes too high, a bookmaker may refuse your bet. You may also run out of capital before a favourite wins.

During the last few minutes before a race, prices can change drastically. Instead of there being just one favourite, a situation can arise where there are joint or even co-favourites. Where you just back the favourite without specifying the name of the horse, your winnings will be greatly reduced if the race is won by a joint or co-favourite. In a situation where there are co-favourites of four, your winnings would only amount to one-quarter of what you had expected. Since the prices of the favourites are low, you are unlikely to recoup your outlay.

Some people apply the system to second favourites because their prices are higher. The problem here is that second favourites win even fewer races than favourites, so the capital needed is greater.

With this system, you are also making no assessment of the runners. By properly considering the chances of each horse, you may discover that another horse is more likely to win the race.

Betting on horses that have travelled a long distance to race

The logic of this is that a trainer wouldn't travel several hundred miles if the horse didn't stand a good chance of winning. The problem with this system is that there may be an equally good horse in the race that has only travelled a short distance. Horses do travel all over the world. British horses are taken to America and France. However, this doesn't mean that they are guaranteed to win.

Betting on horses that have an advantage on the draw

With a lot of British racecourses, the draw can have an effect on the race. Horses starting in certain positions in the stalls have an advantage over others. By combining your assessment of horses with this knowledge, it is possible to select several horses that have a good chance of winning. Instead of backing the horses to win, bets of combination tricasts are placed.

A tricast is predicting which horses will finish first, second and third in the correct order. For a small outlay, the returns are potentially huge.

A particularly good time of the year to play this bet is in the summer months when the ground has dried out and the form is starting to show through. At this time of year it is much easier to assess the horses. You do not have to worry quite so much about the going and you have lots of previous races on which to make your judgement.

In the 1980s bookmakers started to lose a lot of money through this system. Many were also offering huge bonuses of around 20 per cent on correct tricasts, which increased their losses. They are now extremely cautious about accepting bets on combination tricasts, particularly where the stakes are large. In order to get your bet accepted, you may need to spread it around several bookmakers.

Effect of the draw at British and Irish racecourses

Ascot: no significant advantage

Ayr: six furlongs in large field – middle numbers; seven furlongs and over – low numbers

Bath: sprints – low numbers

Beverley: five-furlong course – high numbers

Brighton: sprints – low numbers

Carlisle: high numbers; however, low numbers are favoured when going is soft

Catterick: low numbers

Chepstow: straight course – high numbers; round course – low numbers

Chester: round course seven and a half furlongs – low numbers

Curragh: high numbers

Doncaster: round course – no advantage; straight course – low numbers

Dundalk: no advantage

Edinburgh: seven furlongs and one-mile races – high numbers

Epsom: up to eight and a half furlongs – low numbers

Fairyhouse: no advantage

Folkestone: straight six-furlong course – low numbers

Galway: high numbers

Goodwood: sprint races – high numbers

Gowran Park: no advantage

Great Yarmouth: straight course – high numbers; round course – low numbers

Hamilton Park: straight course – middle to high numbers:

Haydock Park: six furlongs to one mile – low numbers: if going soft on straight course – high numbers

Kempton Park: round course – high numbers

Killarney: no advantage

Laytown: no advantage

Leicester: straight course up to one mile – middle to high numbers (even more so on soft ground)

Leopardstown: slight advantage to low numbers

Lingfield Park: straight course – high numbers if going is heavy, otherwise low numbers

Newbury: no advantage

Newcastle: no advantage

Newmarket: no advantage

Nottingham: straight course – high numbers; round course – low numbers

Pontefract: sprints – low numbers

Redcar: sprints – high numbers

Ripon: straight course – low numbers; round course – high numbers

Salisbury: if going is soft – low numbers

Sandown Park: five-furlong course – high numbers when going is soft

Thirsk: straight course – high numbers; round course – low numbers

Warwick: races up to eight furlongs – high numbers (more marked when going is soft)

Windsor: sprints – high numbers; on soft ground – low numbers

Wolverhampton: no advantage

York: soft ground – low numbers; over seven furlongs – low numbers

Price

Look for horses that offer good value prices. Finding 10/1 winners will give you bigger profits than odds-on horses.

Summary

Concentrate your efforts on a few races each day.

Assess the recent form of a horse.

Place emphasis on the speed of a horse.

Avoid betting on horses that have moved up a class.

Avoid unproven jockeys.

Look for horses that have run recently.

Take account of the draw.

Bear in mind the quality of a horse's previous opponents – an easy win last time out may just be the result of poor opposition.

Be cautious at the beginning of the season and make small bets. Once the form is established, increase stakes. Make bigger bets towards the end of a season when the form is more reliable.

Avoid low-grade races, courses and horses. There will be more information on the best horses that will help you to make a better decision.

Look for horses that offer value bets.

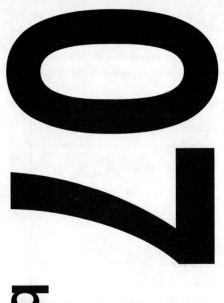

07

blackjack

In this chapter you will learn:
- about the history of blackjack
- about different types of blackjack
- about the bets
- how to play
- basic strategy.

What is blackjack?

Blackjack is a card game played with several decks, commonly four, six or eight. Standard 52-card decks are used. It is based on the game of 21 (pontoon). Rules may vary in different casinos, so always check them before you start playing. You play only against the dealer who plays for the casino. The other players' hands do not affect your game. To win you need to beat the dealer's hand up to a score not exceeding 21. It is played on a semi-circular layout. The software shuffles and deals the cards, pays out winning bets and collects the losing bets. The cards are usually shuffled after each game.

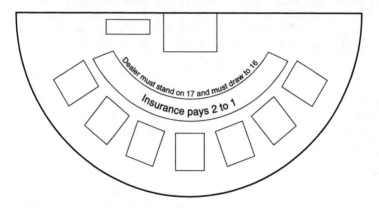

figure 7.1 betting layout for blackjack

The history of blackjack

Playing cards were probably invented in China. The earliest cards were domino cards that represented the scores thrown by a pair of dice, in a similar way to domino tiles. Chinese money cards evolved into modern playing cards. They had four suits that included coins, strings of coins, myriad strings and tens of myriad strings.

Playing cards, similar to those used today, arrived in Europe in the 1370s. They originally had 52-card decks and suits of swords, polo sticks, cups and coins. Each suit had the numbers 1 to 10 and three court cards, which the Europeans changed into kings, knights and valets. Later, queens replaced knights. There were many design changes. The symbols on the cards varied with different cultures. The suits of hearts, spades, diamonds and clubs come from French cards and have continued to be used to the present day.

After the arrival of playing cards in Europe, new games were continually being invented and adapted. Rules were rarely written down. Along with the games went gambling.

Blackjack is derived from the game of 21. It was not very popular when it was first introduced to American casinos. To increase interest, odds of 10 to 1 were offered for a hand comprising an ace and one of the black jacks, giving the game the name blackjack. The game became popular when researchers found that it was possible to overcome the casino's advantage by using a basic strategy. The basic strategy was developed from computer simulations of the game to find the best moves to make depending on the cards dealt. Roger Baldwin published the *Optimum Strategy in Blackjack* in 1956 In 1962, Edward Thorp published *Beat the Dealer* containing card counting techniques. Card counting is a method of play based on the number of cards of certain values left in the shoe (the box from which the cards are dealt). By using a card counting system players can overcome the house advantage (a more detailed description of card counting is given on page 120). Julian Braun added to this research by developing the basic strategy and other card counting techniques. Casinos try to deter card counters by using multiple decks, frequent shuffling and surveillance of players. If they suspect that a winning player is using a card counting system they will often bar the player.

Basics of the game

Card values

All the cards from 2 to 10 inclusive have their face value. So a 2 is worth two and a 6 is worth six and so on. The court cards (kings, queens and jacks) have a value of 10. The value of an ace depends on the total score. When an ace is initially dealt, its value is 11. If a player's hand that contains an ace were to exceed a score of 21, the ace then has a value of one.

Scoring

The value of each card in a hand is added to give the player's score.

16 20

19 21

figure 7.2 blackjack scores

Blackjack

Blackjack is the highest hand possible and, despite its name, has nothing specifically to do with the jacks in the pack. Blackjack is made with any ace and any other card with a value of 10. It can only be made with the first two cards dealt in a hand. It makes no difference whether blackjack is made with a 10 or a court card. A, 10, is equal to A, K. Blackjack beats all other hands, except for a dealer blackjack, when it is a tie or standoff (bets are not lost).

figure 7.3 ways of making blackjack

Although the total score of blackjack is 21, it beats a score of 21 made up with other combinations of cards, for example, three sevens.

If you have blackjack your bet is immediately paid at odds of 3/2 (one and a half to one) unless the dealer's face-up card is an ace or worth 10. In this case, you would have to wait for the outcome of the dealer's hand.

Because only your first two cards can make blackjack, if you receive an ace and a card worth 10 after splitting, you will not have blackjack.

How to play

The cards are shuffled. In order to play, players must make an initial bet by placing sufficient chips in the betting box. The player is dealt two cards face up. The dealer also receives two cards – one face up and one face down. The dealer's card that is not revealed to the players is called the hole card.

Players judge their chances of beating the dealer with the cards they hold and the card shown in the dealer's hand. The cards you have compared to the card in the dealer's hand will determine what you do next. You have several options. You can stand (take no further cards); take more cards to try to improve your score (hit); split your cards into two hands by making an additional bet; or you can double your additional bet. With some online casinos there will be a time limit for you to make your decision. If you do not act within the time limit, it will be assumed that you want to stand.

You can take as many cards as you like to improve your score, but if your score exceeds 21, you lose and your cards will be cleared away. Your bet loses and will be removed. You still lose even if the dealer's hand exceeds 21. A tie or standoff occurs only if both scores are equal and do not exceed 21. Once you are satisfied that you have sufficient cards to beat the dealer's eventual score, you should 'stand' (take no more cards).

After the player's hand has been dealt with, the dealer's hand is played. There are rules that determine the dealer's action. If his score is 16 or less, he must take a card. If his score goes above 21, he has lost and all winning bets are paid. Once he reaches 17 or over he must stand (he can't take any more cards). If the player has beaten the dealer's score, he is paid. If you tie with the dealer, your bet is a standoff (not lost). If your score is lower, you lose.

Options

Depending on the initial value of the cards dealt, you have several options available to you.

Doubling

You may double your initial bet. Rules vary as to when you can double, so always check first. Whether or not doubling your bet is a wise move depends on the dealer's score (see Table 7.1).

Splitting

After two cards have been dealt, you have the options of splitting them into two separate hands. An additional bet equal to your initial bet can be made. (See Table 7.1 for the best option.) If two aces are split into two hands, only one extra card can be taken. If you split two aces and then get a 10-value card – this is not blackjack as you can only have blackjack after two cards have been dealt. Instead, you have a score of 21.

Insurance

Insurance is an additional bet you can make if you have blackjack and the dealer's first card is an ace. Here, you make a further bet equal to half your original stake. If the dealer has blackjack, your original bet loses but your insurance bet is paid at odds of 2/1. If the dealer does not have blackjack, you lose the insurance bet, but your original bet is paid at 3/2.

If you have blackjack and the dealer has an ace, you will be asked if you want to take insurance. When you take insurance, the outcome is the same whether the dealer has blackjack or not. Your net winnings are even money. Some casinos automatically pay you even money as soon as you take insurance. It is generally more advantageous for the player to not take insurance as there is a greater chance that the dealer will make another score and not get blackjack.

Odds paid

If both the dealer and the player have the same score, the bet is a standoff (not lost).

If a player wins with a score of 21 with his first two cards only (blackjack) the odds are 3/2.

If the player beats the dealer on any other score, the odds are 1/1.

Insurance pays 2/1.

Where to place bets

The table is marked with boxes where bets can be placed. These may be rectangular or round (see Figure 7.1). You can bet on as many boxes as you like, up to the table maximum. You can either play yourself or bet on other players' hands. Chips must be placed in the correct position:

- for single bets, chips should be placed in the box
- for split bets, chips should be placed on the line of the box
- for doubled bets, chips should be placed behind the original stake
- for double split bets, chips should be placed behind original stakes on the line.

Variations on the basic game of blackjack

Some casinos offer additional bets on blackjack. Often, though, they are poor-value bets.

Surrender blackjack

This gives you the opportunity to cut your losses when you have a poor hand. After your first two cards have been dealt you have the option to discontinue playing your hand and surrender half of your stake. However, if the dealer has blackjack then you lose all your stake.

Over/under 13

This is an additional bet. You can bet that your first two cards will be either over or under 13. If they score exactly 13 both bets lose. Odds of even money are paid. If you are using a system for counting tens, you can use this information to your advantage and make this additional bet when the shoe is rich in tens.

Multiple-action blackjack

In multiple-action blackjack you keep the same hand for three games and the dealer keeps the same up card throughout. A poor hand may mean three losses but a good hand may lead to three wins.

Basic strategy

Blackjack has an average house advantage of 5.6 per cent. Basic strategy is a method of playing blackjack that can reduce the house advantage to zero. This strategy has been developed by using computer programs to simulate games and to calculate the best action to take for all the different combinations of card dealt.

To use basic strategy you need to memorize the correct action for each combination of cards. Table 7.1 shows the best moves to make depending on what cards are held.

C take a card; – stand; D double; S split									
Player's hand	Dealer's card								
	2	3	4	5	6	7	8	9	10	Ace
8	C	C	C	C	C	C	C	C	C	C
9	C	D	D	D	D	C	C	C	C	C
10	D	D	D	D	D	D	D	D	C	C
11	D	D	D	D	D	D	D	D	D	D
12	C	C	–	–	–	C	C	C	C	C
13	–	–	–	–	–	C	C	C	C	C
14	–	–	–	–	–	C	C	C	C	C
15	–	–	–	–	–	C	C	C	C	C
16	–	–	–	–	–	C	C	C	C	C
Ace 2	C	C	C	C	D	D	C	C	C	C
Ace 3	C	C	C	D	D	C	C	C	C	C
Ace 4	C	C	D	D	D	C	C	C	C	C
Ace 5	C	C	D	D	D	C	C	C	C	C
Ace 6	C	D	D	D	D	C	C	C	C	C
Ace 7	–	–	–	–	–	–	–	C	C	C
Ace 8	–	–	–	–	–	–	–	–	–	–
Ace 9	–	–	–	–	–	–	–	–	–	–
Ace Ace	S	S	S	S	S	S	S	S	S	S
2 2	S	S	S	S	S	S	C	C	C	C
3 3	S	S	S	S	S	S	C	C	C	C
4 4	C	C	C	C	C	C	C	C	C	C
6 6	S	S	S	S	S	C	C	C	C	C
7 7	S	S	S	S	S	S	C	C	C	C
8 8	S	S	S	S	S	S	S	S	S	–
9 9	S	S	S	S	S	–	S	S	–	–
10 10	–	–	–	–	–	–	–	–	–	–

table 7.1 the best moves to make in blackjack

Card counting

If you have played blackjack offline, you may have used card-counting techniques to calculate when the shoe is rich in tens. When this situation arises, the dealer has a greater chance of losing. However, with online blackjack the cards are shuffled after each game, which means that card-counting strategies will not work.

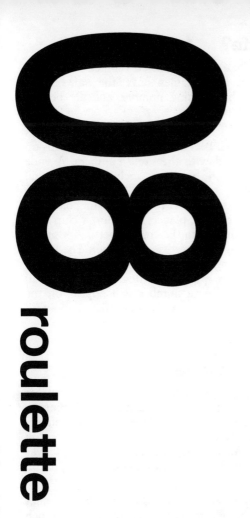

08

roulette

In this chapter you will learn:
- the history of roulette
- about different types of roulette
- about different types of bet
- how to play
- how online roulette differs from traditional roulette.

What is roulette?

Two main versions of the game are played online – American and European roulette. Both games have the same basic principle of predicting the winning number but the betting layout and wheel are different.

Players bet on which number the ball will land in after it has been spun around the wheel. Bets are made by placing chips on the layout, which is marked with the same numbers. A wide choice of different bets can be made including individual numbers and groups of up to 18 numbers. Bets made on the winning number are paid at set odds. To start playing, onscreen chips are bought. To make a bet, players touch on a chip with their mouse pointer and drag it to the correct betting position. A timer indicates how long a player has left to bet. The ball is spun from the last winning number. So if the last winning number was 36, on the next spin the starting point of the ball will be number 36. The winning number will appear on the screen. The winning bets are automatically calculated and paid by the software.

The history of roulette

Gambling games using spinning wheels have been played for thousands of years. Some of the earliest games using spinning wheels date back to Ancient Rome and Greece. Roman soldiers would mark sections on a chariot wheel, spin it and bet on where it would stop. In Ancient Greece, the same principle was applied to shields that were marked with sections and spun on spears.

The horizontal spinning wheel that forms the basic equipment for game of roulette is thought to have been invented by French mathematician Blaise Pascal in the 17th century. He was experimenting with perpetual motion devices. The wheel is thought to have been a result of these experiments. Roulette wheels are mounted on a spindle and, much like flywheels, a small push on the wheel is enough to keep the wheel spinning for a considerable length of time.

Games that resemble roulette emerged in England in the 18th century. In 1720 a game called roly-poly was invented. It was played with a ball that was spun round a horizontal rotating wheel. It became extremely popular and was played in taverns and gaming houses. In 1739 and 1740 gaming acts were passed banning the game. To get round the ban a simplified version of the game was invented called even odd. Alternate sections of the wheel were marked with 'E' and 'O' respectively. Players would bet on whether E or O would be spun. By 1745 the game of even odd was also banned.

Double-zero roulette

Double-zero roulette is a version of roulette that incorporates two zeros. It first emerged during the 18th century in France. The name 'roulette' is French meaning small wheel. It was probably based on a French street game that was played on a board with 36 numbers on it. The numbers were marked on lots that were placed in a bag. One of the lots would be drawn from the bag to determine the winning number. The wheel most likely replaced the lots with the betting layout being retained.

By 1796 double-zero roulette wheels had been introduced to Paris. They resembled modern double-zero wheels with the numbers 1 to 36, one zero and a double zero. The colour of the zeros differed, instead of green, zero was coloured red and the double zero was coloured black. The rules regarding the outcome of outside bets also varied. Bets on red lost if zero was spun and bets on black lost if double zero was spun. Later, the zeros were changed to the colour green. The rules concerning the outcome of outside bets when zero is spun were also amended.

The betting layout also differed from the modern one. It resembled a French roulette betting layout with the outside bets on either side of the numbers. Later, the more compact modern layouts emerged with the outside bets on one side only.

These double-zero wheels were taken to the United States by settlers in the 19th century. Casinos opened in New Orleans and along the Mississippi River. Gambling spread to the west as settlers moved there with wagon trains. When gold was discovered in California in 1848, gambling flourished in the prospecting camps. San Francisco, which became a huge tented city, had over 1000 gambling houses where gold was the currency. Roulette was one of the most popular games.

Lack of legislation controlling the games resulted in some unscrupulous operators introducing wheels with 31 pockets, which featured the numbers 1 to 28, one zero, a double zero and an eagle. Payout odds for a winning number were just 26/1 giving the operators a massive 12.9 per cent house advantage compared with 5.26 per cent on a regular double-zero wheel. Nowadays double-zero wheels are used on American roulette played in the United States.

Single-zero roulette (French roulette)

Frenchmen François and Louis Blanc invented roulette with a single zero in 1842. They removed the double zero from the wheel and haphazardly rearranged the numbers 1 to 36. Despite removing one of the pockets, they kept the payout odds for a winning number at 35/1. This cut the house advantage to just 2.7 per cent, which proved extremely popular with gamblers. Since gambling had been made illegal in France in 1837, they introduced the game to Bad-Homburg in Germany. It was a great success. When gaming was outlawed in Germany, François and his son Camille brought the game to Monte Carlo.

In 1857 Prince Charles III of Monaco decided to introduce gambling to the principality to boost its finances. Gambling had just been outlawed in Germany. This prompted Leblanc to bring his game of single-zero roulette to Monte Carlo. Monte Carlo had the monopoly on roulette until 1933.

English roulette

English roulette is a version of roulette that uses a single-zero wheel and a smaller betting layout – similar to the size of an American roulette layout. To confuse matters English roulette is often called American roulette. You may also hear it called single-zero American roulette. It is played mostly in the UK and continental Europe. English roulette has evolved from combining some elements of French roulette with American roulette. French roulette using the single-zero wheel was introduced to England in the 1960s. French roulette needs two or three dealers. In contrast, American roulette can be operated by just one dealer and is a much faster game than French roulette. To increase profits, casinos started replacing French roulette tables with English roulette. The betting layout was modified so that it could be used with the single-zero wheel. English roulette also uses the French names for most of the bets. A straight up (a bet on a single number), for example, is called an 'en plein' (pronounced 'on plan') and a split (a bet on two numbers) is a 'cheval' (pronounced 'shevale'). English roulette has led to the decline of French roulette.

Aussie roulette and rapid roulette

In 2000 a new form of roulette was introduced called rapid roulette. It was based on Aussie roulette, a slot machine version of the game that was played in Australian casinos. Aussie roulette was not particularly popular with traditional roulette players because they preferred the human factor of having a dealer spin the ball. In 1999 Crown Casino Australia and Stargames started to develop a semi-automated version of roulette that would combine both elements of traditional and Aussie roulette. This hybrid was called rapid roulette. Rapid roulette uses a traditional roulette wheel and dealer to generate the winning numbers. Versions using the single-zero wheel and the double-zero wheel exist. The dealer also handles the buy-ins. The baize betting layout was replaced with computer terminals that are arranged around the roulette table so that the players can see the ball being spun. The new game allows bets to be placed without the pushing and shoving associated with traditional roulette. It also allows for varied stakes. Rapid roulette has soared in popularity and is now played in casinos around the world.

Online versions of roulette

European roulette

European roulette uses a single-zero wheel. The numbers 0 to 36 are arranged around the wheel on numbered compartments. Each number is coloured. Zero is green and the other numbers are either red or black. American roulette uses a wheel with two zeros – zero and double zero. The ball is spun in the opposite direction to that of the wheel. As the ball loses momentum it slows down and eventually drops into one of the numbered slots. Figure 8.1 shows the European wheel and betting layout.

American roulette

American roulette uses a wheel with two zeros. The numbers are arranged so that consecutive numbers are on opposite sides of the wheel. For example, number 1 is opposite number 2. On one side of the layout, there is a double line between the outside bets and the numbers. This double line denotes where street and double street bets should be placed (see bets on page 129). Figure 8.2 shows the American wheel and betting layout.

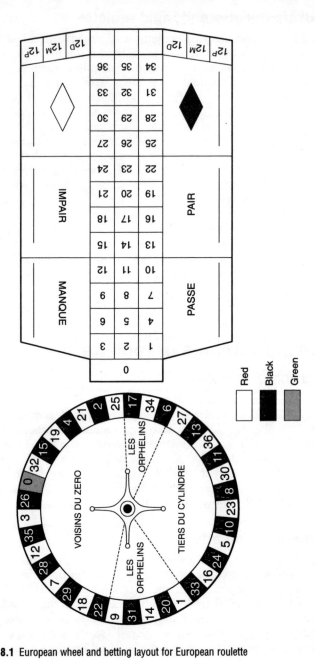

figure 8.1 European wheel and betting layout for European roulette

Why play roulette?

Roulette has a low house advantage compared to other games. On a single-zero wheel, the house advantage is 2.7 per cent. Blackjack in contrast has a house advantage of 5.6 per cent – double that on roulette, as the casinos takes a bigger profit on blackjack.

The high payout odds for a winning number on roulette make it possible to quickly accumulate winnings. A winning number pays odds of 35/1 whereas blackjack only pays 2/1. By re-betting the winnings on roulette it is possible to win over £1000 in just two spins of a roulette wheel.

Betting on roulette

Roulette offers the player a wide choice of bets. They are bets on either one number or combinations of numbers. In addition, bets can be made on the characteristic of a number, which includes its colour (red or black), whether it is an even or odd number and whether it is a high or a low number. With some casinos it is also possible to bet on sections of the wheel. Other bets, called 'completes', allow the maximum stake on all bets associated with a number.

The bets are placed by the positioning of the chips on the layout. Bets may be placed as soon as the dealer gives the instruction 'place your bets'. When time has run out for placing bets, the dealer will announce 'no more bets'.

Bets on the part of the layout marked with the numbers 0 to 36 are called 'inside bets'. Bets on the characteristic of the number like low, even, red, black, odd and high are called outside bets.

Bet values

The game software will let you specify the value of your 'chips'.

The bets

Straight up (en plein)

A bet on any one of the numbers from 0 to 36, including zero and double zero. The chip should be placed directly on top of the desired number on the layout. It wins only if that number is spun. Odds paid are 35/1.

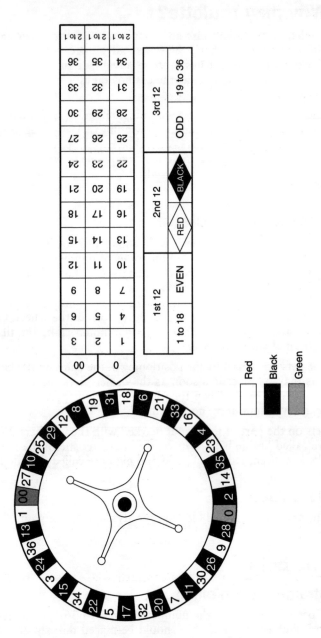

figure 8.2 American wheel and betting layout for American roulette

Split (cheval)

A bet on two adjacent numbers on the layout. The bet is placed on the centre of the line between the two numbers. It wins if either of the two numbers is spun. Odds paid are 17/1.

Street (transversale plein)

A bet on three adjacent numbers across the layout. It wins if any of the three numbers is spun. Odds paid are 11/1. The bet is placed on the double line between the numbers and the dozens.

Corner (carré)

A bet on four adjacent numbers on the layout. The chip is placed on the cross section of the line where the four numbers meet. It wins if any of the four numbers is spun. Odds paid are 8/1.

First four

This is also a bet on four numbers. The first four is a bet on the numbers 0, 1, 2, and 3. It can cause some confusion because of its name. Despite its name it loses if number four is spun. It is placed on the corner of the layout where numbers one and zero and the first dozen meet. It wins if any of the four numbers 0, 1, 2 or 3 wins. Odds of 8/1 are paid.

First five

This bet can only be played on roulette with two zeros and is a bet the five numbers 0, 00, 1, 2 and 3. Despite its name, again, it loses if the numbers four or five are spun. It is placed on the lines where zero, double zero and two meet. Odds paid are 6/1. This bet is best avoided as it is the least profitable from a player's point of view. It gives it the casino a house advantage of 7.89 per cent – much higher than the other bets on double-zero roulette, which give a house advantage of 5.26 per cent.

Double street (sixainne or transversale simple)

A bet on six adjacent numbers across the layout. The chip is placed on the double line at the side of the layout at the cross-section of the middle line of the six numbers. Odds paid are 5/1.

Quatro

Some betting layouts incorporate bets on a quarter of the numbers. The first quarter is the numbers 1–9 inclusive, the second is the numbers 10–18 inclusive, the third is the numbers 19–27 and the fourth is the numbers 28–36. Bets are placed in the appropriate box. Odds paid are 3 to 1. Bets lose if zero is spun.

Dozen

A bet on a group of 12 consecutive numbers. There are three dozens. Numbers 1–12, 13–24 and 25–36 inclusive. Bets are placed in the appropriate box. The bet wins if any of the 12 numbers is spun. Odds paid are 2/1. All bets on the dozens lose if zero is spun.

Column

A bet on a group of 12 numbers running in a column along the table. There are three columns. Bets are placed in the box at the base of the column. The bet wins if any number in the column is spun. Odds paid are 2/1. All bets on the columns lose if zero is spun.

Even chances/outside bets (chance simple)

These are bets on a certain characteristic of the number spun, whether it is red, black, even, odd, high or low. Bets are placed in the box marked with that characteristic. The bet wins if the appropriate characteristic is spun. Odds paid are evens (1/1). Before playing these bets, check what happens if zero is spun as some casinos have different rules. In British casinos, if zero is spun players lose half their stake.

Low

This is a bet on the low numbers on the wheel. It will win if any of the numbers 1 to 18 inclusive is spun.

High

This is a bet on the high numbers on the wheel. It will win if any of the numbers 19 to 36 inclusive is spun.

Red

This is a bet on the numbers coloured red on the wheel. It will win if any of the red numbers is spun.

Black

This is a bet on the numbers coloured black on the wheel. It will win if any of the black numbers is spun.

Even

This is a bet on the even numbers on the wheel. It will win if any of the even numbers is spun.

Odd

This is a bet on the odd numbers on the wheel. It will win if any of the odd numbers is spun.

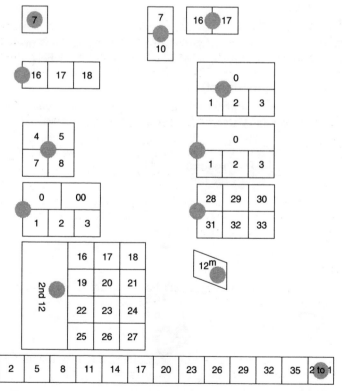

figure 8.3 different kinds of bet and where to place them

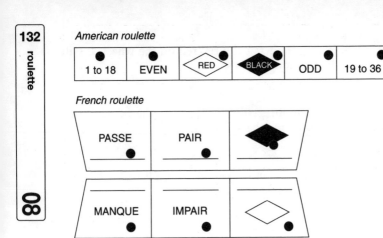

American roulette

French roulette

figure 8.4 where to place even-chance bets

Speciality bets

There are a number of bets than can be played on European roulette and these cover particular sections of the wheel.

Voisins (neighbour bet)

A bet on five numbers straight up that are adjacent to one another on the wheel. A bet on 5 and the neighbours (et les voisins) on a single-zero wheel is a bet on 5 and the two numbers either side of it on the wheel (a straight up on the numbers 16, 24, 5, 10 and 23). Seventeen and the neighbours would be an en plein bet on each of the numbers 2, 25, 17, 34 and 6.

figure 8.5 neighbours of 17

12	35	3	26	**0**	32	15	19	4
5	24	16	33	**1**	20	14	31	9
15	19	4	21	**2**	25	17	34	6
7	28	12	35	**3**	26	0	32	15
0	32	15	19	**4**	21	2	25	17
30	8	23	10	**5**	24	16	33	1
2	25	17	34	**6**	27	13	36	11
9	22	18	29	**7**	28	12	35	3
13	36	11	30	**8**	23	10	5	24
1	20	14	31	**9**	22	18	29	7
11	30	8	23	**10**	5	24	16	33
6	27	13	36	**11**	30	8	23	10
18	29	7	28	**12**	35	3	26	0
17	34	6	27	**13**	36	11	30	8
16	33	1	20	**14**	31	9	22	18
3	26	0	32	**15**	19	4	21	2
23	10	5	24	**16**	33	1	20	14
4	21	2	25	**17**	34	6	27	13
14	31	9	22	**18**	29	7	28	12
26	0	32	15	**19**	4	21	2	25
24	16	33	1	**20**	14	31	9	22
32	15	19	4	**21**	2	25	17	34
20	14	31	9	**22**	18	29	7	28
36	11	30	8	**23**	10	5	24	16
8	23	10	5	**24**	16	33	1	20
19	4	21	2	**25**	17	34	6	27
28	12	35	3	**26**	0	32	15	19
25	17	34	6	**27**	13	36	11	30
22	18	29	7	**28**	12	35	3	26
31	9	22	18	**29**	7	28	12	35
27	13	36	11	**30**	8	23	10	5
33	1	20	14	**31**	9	22	18	29
35	3	26	0	**32**	15	19	4	21
10	5	24	16	**33**	1	20	14	31
21	2	25	17	**34**	6	27	13	36
29	7	28	12	**35**	3	26	0	32
34	6	27	13	**36**	11	30	8	23

table 8.1 neighbours on a European wheel

24	36	13	1	**00**	27	10	25	29
3	24	36	13	**1**	00	27	10	25
4	23	35	14	**2**	0	28	9	26
5	22	34	15	**3**	24	36	13	1
6	21	33	16	**4**	23	35	14	2
7	20	32	17	**5**	22	34	15	3
8	19	31	18	**6**	21	33	16	4
9	26	30	11	**7**	20	32	17	5
10	25	29	12	**8**	19	31	18	6
14	2	0	28	**9**	26	30	11	7
13	1	00	27	**10**	25	29	12	8
28	9	26	30	**11**	7	20	32	17
27	10	25	29	**12**	8	19	31	18
15	3	24	36	**13**	1	00	27	10
16	4	23	35	**14**	2	0	28	9
17	5	22	34	**15**	3	24	36	13
18	6	21	33	**16**	4	23	35	14
11	7	20	32	**17**	5	22	34	15
12	8	19	31	**18**	6	21	33	16
25	29	12	8	**19**	31	18	6	21
26	30	11	7	**20**	32	17	5	22
19	31	18	6	**21**	33	16	4	23
20	32	17	5	**22**	34	15	3	24
21	33	16	4	**23**	35	14	2	0
22	34	15	3	**24**	36	13	1	00
1	00	27	10	**25**	29	12	8	19
2	0	28	9	**26**	30	11	7	20
36	13	1	00	**27**	10	25	29	12
35	14	2	0	**28**	9	26	30	11
00	27	10	25	**29**	12	8	19	31
0	28	9	26	**30**	11	7	20	32
29	12	8	19	**31**	18	6	21	33
30	11	7	20	**32**	17	5	22	34
31	18	6	21	**33**	16	4	23	35
32	17	5	22	**34**	15	3	24	36
33	16	4	23	**35**	14	2	0	28
34	15	3	24	**36**	13	1	00	27

table 8.2 neighbours on an American wheel

Bets covering sections of the wheel

There are a number of bets designed to cover sections of the
single-zero roulette wheel using the minimum number of chips.
The wheel shows the names of each section of the wheel (see
Figure 8.1).

Tiers du cylindre

This bet covers the section of numbers between 27 and 33. It
includes the numbers 27, 13, 36, 11, 30, 8, 23, 10, 5, 24, 16,
33. It is often referred to as tiers. This bet uses just six chips to
cover this section of numbers. The bets placed are six splits
(chevals) on the numbers 5/8, 10/11, 13/16, 23/24, 27/30,
33/36. A winning number on this section of the wheel wins 17
chips and loses five chips. The odds for this bet work out at
11/1.

Voisins du zero

This bet covers the section of the wheel from 22 to 25. It
includes the numbers 22, 8, 29, 7, 28, 12, 35, 3, 26, 0, 32, 15,
19, 4, 21, 2 and 25. The bet is made with nine chips. The bets
made are 0/2/3 (two chips) street. Splits (chevals) of 4/7, 12/15,
18/21, 19/22, 32/35 and a four-number bet 25/29 (two pieces).
If the numbers 0, 2 or 3 is spun, 22 chips are won and seven
chips are lost. If numbers 25, 26, 28 or 29 is spun, 16 chips are
won and seven are lost. If any of the other numbers is spun 17
chips are won and eight are lost.

Les orphélins (the orphans)

This is a bet on the sections of the wheel that are not covered by
the tiers and the voisins du zero. It covers two opposite sections
of the wheel. The numbers covered are 9, 31, 14, 20, 1, 6, 34
and 17. The bet is made with five chips. It consists of number 1
straight up and the splits 6/9, 14/17, 17/20, 31/34. If number 1
is spun, 35 chips are won and four chips lost. If number 17 wins
34 chips are won and three chips are lost. If 6, 9, 14, 20, 31or
34 is spun, 17 chips are won and four chips are lost.

Complete bet

This is a bet that allows a player to bet the maximum stake on
a number. Suppose you want to bet the maximum possible
amount on 0, as well as a straight up, it is possible to play all
the other bets associated with 0. These are the splits 0/1, 0/2 and
0/3; the streets 0/1/2 and 0/2/3 and the first four 0/1/2/3.

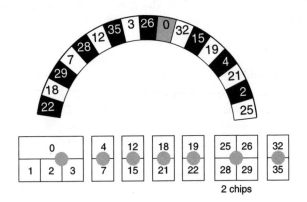

2 chips

Les oprhélins

 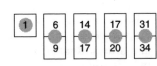

Tiers du cylindre

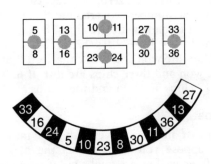

figure 8.6 bets covering sections of the wheel

If the maximum bet for a straight up is £1000, the maximum stake on the other bets will be:

split, £2000
street, £3000
corner, £4000.

By betting with £1000 chips, 17 chips will be needed to make the maximum possible bet:

one straight up = £1000
three splits = £6000
two streets = £6000
first four = £4000.
total stake = £17000 or 17 × £1000 chips.

The completes only takes account of the inside bets. The outside bets associated with black, even, low, the dozen and the columns are not included.

The number of chips required to place a complete varies depending on the number. This is because each number has a different number of bets associated with it, depending on its position on the betting layout. For example, there are four splits around number 2 and only three associated with 0. Each number therefore needs a different number of chips for a complete to be played. Table 8.3 gives the number of maximum stake chips needed for a complete bet and the payout for a winning number.

Winning number	Number of chips of maximum stake	Payout for a winning number (in chips)
0	17	235
1 and 3	27	297
2	36	396
1st and 3rd column from 4 to 31 and 6 to 33	30	294
Middle column from 5 to 32	40	392
34 and 36	18	198
35	24	264

table 8.3 complete staking chart

It is also possible to bet on complete dozens. The number of chips is as follows:

first dozen – 136 chips
second dozen – 140 chips
third dozen – 120 chips.

Number and the chevals

This is a bet straight up and the associated splits (chevals). It is a five-chip bet. The numbers in the second column from 2 to 32 have four chevals. Numbers 34 and 36 have two chevals. All the other numbers have three chevals. Where there are fewer than four chevals, the extra chip(s) is put on as a straight-up bet. For example, 14 and the chevals comprises the following bets. Straight up number 14 – one chip; cheval 11/14 – one chip; cheval 13/14 – one chip; cheval 14/15– one chip and cheval 14/17 – one chip.

Where there are only three chevals, the extra chip is put on the number. Number 7 and the chevals comprises the bets:

straight up – two chips
cheval 4/7 – one chip
cheval 7/8 – one chip
cheval 7/10 – one chip.

Name of bet (US/Europe)	Amount of numbers covered	Odds
Straight/En plein	1	35/1
Split/Cheval	2	17/1
Street/Transversale plein	3	11/1
Corner/Carré	4	8/1
Double street/Sixainne or transversale simple	6	5/1
First five	5	5/1
Dozen	12	2/1
Column	12	2/1
Low/Manqué	18	1/1 (evens)
High/Passé	18	1/1 (evens)
Red	18	1/1 (evens)
Black	18	1/1 (evens)
Odd	18	1/1 (evens)
Even	18	1/1 (evens)

table 8.4 table of odds for roulette

Zero

Zero and double zero are numbers, just like 1 to 36. A straight-up chip is paid at 35/1. However, zero and double zero have an effect on the outside bets. Depending on the casino's rules there is some variation in what happen to the outside bets when zero is spun.

When zero is spun, the outside bets lose half of their stake. If, for example, you had a bet of £10 on red and zero is spun, you will lose £5.

In other casinos, there is the en prison rule. The bets are held for a further spin. If on the next spin, they win, the stake is returned to the player. If they lose, the stake is lost. For example, if you had a bet of £10 on black and zero is spun, you need to wait until the next spin to find out what will happen to your bet. If a black number is spun, your £10 bet will be returned to you. If red is spun, your bet will lose.

Calculating payouts

Example

Your winning bets may be as follows:

    three sixainnes at 5/1
    one carré at 8/1
    two chevals at 17/1
    four en pleins at 35/1

$(3 \times 5) + 8 + (2 \times 17) + (4 \times 35) = 197$

These bets total 197 chips

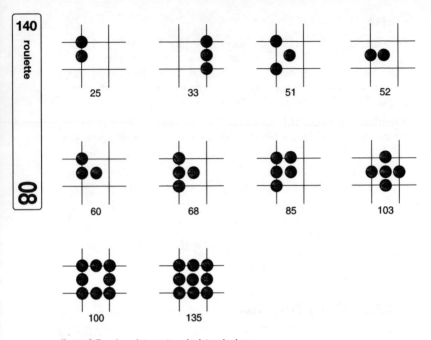

figure 8.7 using pictures to calculate winnings

Why players lose

Lack of education

Many players learn how to play the games from other players. They pick up bad habits and get misinformed about the chances of winning.

Playing the slow death

One of the most common mistakes made by players is to play what casinos call the 'slow death'. These players do not understand the concept of the house advantage.

This tends to happen a lot with bets on the dozens. A player will typically bet on all three dozens on one spin. Because they get paid out they think they are winning. They don't understand that they are only breaking even. Then zero comes up and they lose all three chips. Even then they still don't understand that they can't possibly win. Such players continue playing until they eventually run out of chips.

Other players opt for a faster form of the slow death. They put a chip on each number and are delighted when they win and get paid. They fail to notice that they are actually losing until they run out of chips.

Relying on the law of averages

Many players rely on the law of averages – that in the long run all numbers will be spun an equal amount of times. However, the law of averages is a fallacy. Consider the tossing of a coin. If a coin lands on heads on the first toss does this mean the second toss will be tails? The answer is possibly since there is a 50 per cent chance that it could land on either side. Suppose you tossed the coin 100 times. What result would you expect? According to the law of averages, it would be 50 times heads and 50 times tails because in the long run it would even out. But just because there is a 50 per cent chance of something happening, it doesn't mean it will happen 50 per cent of the time. The coin does not know what the previous result was. Each subsequent toss is totally unrelated to the previous toss. There is actually no reason why you couldn't throw 100 heads or 100 tails in a row.

With roulette some players bet on numbers that have failed to appear because the law of averages says that they should eventually be spun. However, it has been known for some numbers not to appear at certain tables for weeks. The roulette wheel has no memory. By waiting for one particular number that has not appeared for a while, you can easily lose a lot of money.

Belief in systems

Many players want to win but are prepared to put very little effort into ensuring that they do win. Many are looking for a quick easy system that is not complicated. This is why they get seduced into playing one of the common systems like the martingale (see later for further details). With these types of system, it is also easy to lose. A system may appear to work over a short time span but this often has more to due with luck.

The martingale

One of the most popular systems is the martingale. This involves doubling the stakes on losing bets and continuing to play until you have a winner. It is commonly used to play on the outside bets (red, black, even, odd, high or low). The way that it works is that the player makes a bet on, for example, red. If this bet loses the stake is then doubled on the next spin. If this wins then the player has won one chip and has recouped his losses on the previous bet. The problem with this system is that the table limit is soon reached, making it impossible to continue to double up. It also requires players to have a large bankroll to make large bets. The reason that so many players think it works is that they try it out and win. However, their win is not due to the system, it is simply due to luck.

How so?

Suppose a table has a minimum bet of £10 and a maximum of £1000. The first bet is £10 on red. If this loses, the next bet is £20. If the player continues to lose, the bets need to be increased to £40, £80, £160, £320, £640. Now the system will fail as the table maximum is £1000 and the player needs to bet £1280 to recoup his losses. This means that a succession of seven black numbers has caused the system to fail. The player has now spent £1270 with no prospect of recouping losses.

Not knowing when to quit

Not knowing when to quit is a huge problem. It is extremely common for players to have big wins but to end up losing all their winnings. It is often due to the player trying to recoup losses by making bigger bets.

House advantage

With single-zero roulette the odds paid for a bet on en plein (one number) are 35/1. However, the true odds are 36/1. So, for each spin the casino has one number working in its favour. The house advantage is 2.7 per cent of the stakes, that is, for every £37 that you bet, the casino is raking off £1.

The casino comes off even better if the player bets on a roulette wheel with two zeros. Now there are 38 numbers but the odds paid are the same for a winning number (35/1). If a player bets a chip on every number, the casino wins two chips on every spin. By adding an extra zero, the casino effectively doubles its profits.

How online roulette differs from traditional roulette

You may have played roulette offline, but there are number of fundamental differences with online roulette that affect playing strategies. The lack of human input with online roulette means that strategies analysing a particular dealer's spin will not work. The number is decided by a random number generator. This makes it virtually impossible to calculate the next winning number. If you want to play roulette, then you should play simply for amusement purposes.

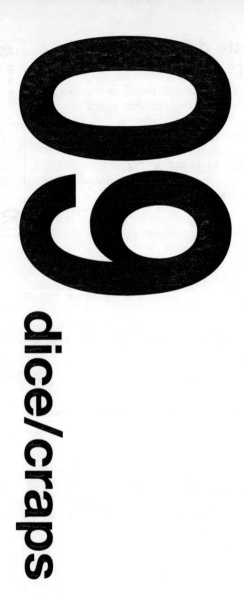

09

dice/craps

In this chapter you will learn:
- the history of dice games
- about bets
- how to play
- how to understand the odds
- about house advantage.

Dice, also known as craps, is a game based on the throws of two dice. Players predict whether or not a winning or a losing score will be thrown. The complex betting layout makes dice appear more difficult than it actually is. The basic game is relatively easy to learn. Although the layout incorporates a wide choice of bets, in practice, only a few are worth playing.

The history of dice games

Dice games are one of the oldest forms of gambling and were originally played with dice fashioned from the knucklebones of sheep. Gambling was very popular in Ancient Rome where various forms of dice game were played. Gradually these games spread across Europe. During the 18th and 19th centuries hazard was a popular game played by the aristocracy. Craps got its name when hazard was introduced to France. Crabs, a pair of ones, was the lowest score. The French misinterpreted the word 'crabs' as craps.

European settlers brought the game to America where it was simplified and became the modern game of craps.

How to play

Two dice are thrown. To calculate the score the number of spots on the uppermost faces are added. See Figure 9.1 for examples.

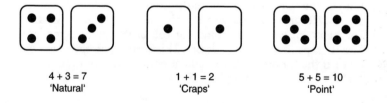

4 + 3 = 7
'Natural'

1 + 1 = 2
'Craps'

5 + 5 = 10
'Point'

figure 9.1 dice scores

The first throw of the dice is called the 'come-out roll'. A first throw of 7 or 11 is a winning score. A throw of 2, 3 or 12 is a losing score (craps). Any other score (4, 5, 6, 8, 9 or 10) means that a point is established. When a point is established, the player will try to make the point by re-throwing the dice any number of times to repeat the original score. If the original score is thrown before a 7 or 11, it is a winning score. If a 7 or 11 is thrown first, it is a losing score.

When it is your turn to be the shooter (the one who throws the dice), you must place a bet on win pass or don't pass (win or don't win). You continue to throw until there is a losing decision (a miss out).

The first throw is called the come-out. If a 7 or 11 is thrown, the bet on the pass (win) line wins (a winning decision) and the bet on don't pass loses. If 2, 3, or 12 (craps) is thrown, the bet on the pass line loses (a losing decision) and the bet on the don't pass line wins.

If a point is established (a score of 4, 5, 6, 8, 9 or 10), the shooter continues rolling the dice. If the point is made (the original score re-thrown), the pass bet wins and the don't pass bet loses. If a 7 or 11 is thrown, the don't pass bet wins and the pass bet loses.

Types of bet

There is a wide range of bets. Try to familiarize yourself with them and learn where they are placed on the layout before you play (see Figure 9.2).

Pass (win) line

Win bets must be placed before the come-out roll. They cannot be removed or reduced after the point is established. It wins if a 7 or 11 is thrown on the come-out roll or if a point is made. It loses if craps (a score of 2, 3, or 12) is thrown on the come-out roll or if the shooter fails to make a point. Odds of even money (1/1) are paid on winning bets.

Don't pass (don't win) line

This is the opposite of pass. The bet must be placed before the come-out roll. After a point is established it can be reduced or removed. The bet wins if craps is thrown on the come-out roll or if the shooter fails to make a point. It loses if 7 or 11 is thrown on the come-out roll or if a point is made.

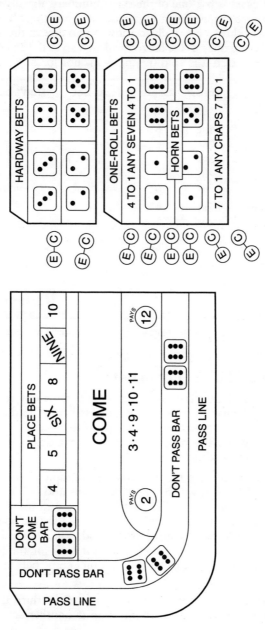

figure 9.2 betting layout for dice

A lot of casinos bar one of the craps numbers, usually either 12 or 2, to give themselves a bigger house advantage. If a score is barred it is shown by an illustration of two dice in the don't win section – two ones if 2 is barred and two sixes if 12 is barred. If a score is barred it is void (neither wins nor loses).

	Throw	Score	Pass bet	Don't pass bet
Example 1	1st	7	wins	loses
Example 2	1st	6*		
	2nd	5		
	3rd	5		
	4th	2		
	5th	6**	wins	loses
Example 3	1st	6*		
	2nd	5		
	3rd	4		
	4th	7**	loses	wins
Example 4	1st		3 (craps)	loses wins
* point established				
**point made				

table 9.1 effect of a sequence of throws on the pass and don't pass bets

Come and don't come bets

These bets allow players who miss the come-out roll to bet. They are similar to pass and don't pass bets. The difference is that they can be placed on any throw of the dice after the come-out roll. When the bet is placed, the next throw of the dice becomes the first throw for the bet.

The rules concerning the win/loss are the same as the pass line. If a 7 or 11 is thrown the come bets wins and don't come bets lose. If craps is thrown the come bets lose and the don't come bets win. Any other number thrown establishes a point. If the point is made the come bets win and don't come bets lose. However, the score need not be the same as for the pass bets. Scores of 2 or 12 may be barred for don't come bets (see section on don't pass bets).

If, for example, a come bet was placed on the third throw and the score is 6, the come bet will win if another score of 6 is thrown before a 7 or 11.

When a come or don't come bet is placed, the dealer will move the bet to the box of the score required. Come bets cannot be reduced or removed after a point is established. Don't come bets may be removed or reduced after a point is established.

Odds bets

These are additional bets that can be made once a point has been established. You must already have a bet on pass, don't pass, come or don't come. The bets are paid out at the true mathematical odds and are worth playing as the house advantage is reduced. However, casinos limit the amount that you can bet. Some allow a bet of up to the amount of your original wager, others allow you to bet double the original wager. Odds bets can be reduced or removed at anytime.

On the come-out roll, come odds bets are 'off' but may be called 'on' by the player and don't come odds bets are 'on'.

Place bet

This is a bet on the individual scores of 4, 5, 6, 8, 9 or 10. It wins if the score selected is thrown before a 7 is rolled. These bets can be made at any time. Place bets are 'off' at the come-out roll unless you call them 'on'. The bets can be increased, decreased, removed or called off at any time.

Buy bet

Buy bets are similar to place bets except that a 5 per cent commission is paid when the bet is placed. The bets are then settled at the true mathematical odds. An easy way to find 5 per cent is to halve the amount of your bet and move the decimal point one place to the left. The bets may be increased, decreased or removed at any time and the commission adjusted accordingly each time.

If your buy bet wins and you leave it on again, you need to pay an additional 5 per cent commission. Buy bets are automatically 'off' on the come-out roll, but may be called 'on' by the player.

Lay bets

Lay bets are the opposite of buy bets. If a 7 is rolled before the number on which a lay bet is wagered, the wager wins at true odds. The wager loses if the number on which a lay bet is wagered rolls before a 7 is rolled.

For a lay bet, the 5 per cent commission is charged on the amount the wager could win (not on the amount wagered as with buy bets). So, if you place a £40 bet on 4, the winnings would be £20 (£40 at 1/2 = £60, £60 – £40 stake = £20). Commission payable is 5 per cent of £20 = £1. You would therefore need to pay £41.

One-roll bets

Some bets are made on just one roll of the dice:

field – for the numbers 2, 3, 4, 9, 10, 11 or 12 to be thrown. It loses if a 5, 6, 7 or 8 is rolled.

hardways – throwing the same number on each die. Hardway four is two deuces, hardway six is two threes, hardway eight is two fours and hardway ten is two fives. A hardway bet is for the numbers 4, 6, 8, or 10 to be rolled hardway. Hardways are 'off' on the come out roll but can be called 'on'.

any seven – for a 7 to be rolled

any craps – the numbers 2, 3 or 12

craps two – number 2 (two ones)

craps twelve – a bet on number 12 (two sixes)

craps three – number 3 (a 2 and a 1)

eleven – number 11 (5 and 6)

horn – this bet is made in units of four. It is for the numbers 2, 3, 11 or 12 being rolled. It is treated as four separate bets on each number

horn high – the same as a horn except that there is one stake unit on each of the numbers and an extra stake unit on any of the numbers that the player nominates. So if number 11 were nominated it would have two stake units on it.

Payout odds		House advantage per cent
Pass line 1/1 even		1/41
Don't pass line 1/1 even		1/4–4.38 depending on numbers barred
Come 1/1 even		1.41
Don't come 1/1 even		1/4–4.38 depending on numbers barred
Odds pass line and come		
4 or 10 2/1 (1/2)*		0
5 or 9 3/2 (2/3)*		0
6 or 8 6/5 (5/6)*		0
*Odds don't pass line and don't come		
Place bets (to win)		
4 or 10 9/5		6.7
5 or 9 7/5		4
6 or 8 7/6		1.5
Buy bets		
4 or 10 2/1		5
5 or 9 3/9		5
6 or 8 6/5		5
Lay bets		
4 or 10 1/2		2.5
5 or 9 2/3		3.2
6 or 8 5/6		4
Field (one bet roll)		
3, 4, 9, 10, 11 1/1		11.11
2 or 12 2/1		5.55
Hardways		
4 or 10 7/1		11.1
6 or 8 9/1		9.09
One-roll bets		
Any seven	4/1	16.67
Any craps (2, 3 or 12)	7/1	11
Craps two	30/1	14
Craps three	15/1	11
Craps twelve	30/1	14
Eleven	15/1	11

table 9.2 dice payout odds and house advantage

Chances of throwing each score

There are 36 ways in which the dice can be thrown. A score of 7 can be made in six different ways and a score of 11 can be made two ways. A point can be established in 24 different ways. There is only one way each of throwing 2 or 12 and two ways to throw 3. Therefore, you stand a fairly good chance of either throwing a natural or establishing a point on the come-out roll.

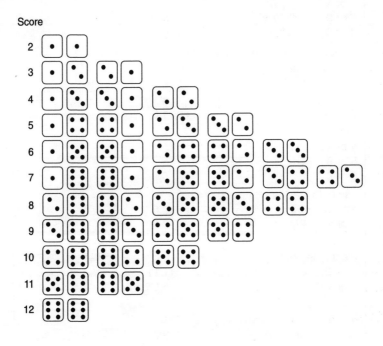

figure 9.3 different ways of making scores

2	2.77%
3	5.55%
4	8.33%
5	11.11%
6	13.88%
7	16.66%
8	13.88%
9	11.11%
10	8.33%
11	5.55%
12	2.77%

table 9.3 chances of throwing each score

Natural 7 or 11	22.22% (8/36)
Point 4, 5, 6, 8, 9, 10	66.66% (24/36)
Craps 2, 3 or 12	11.11% (4/36)

table 9.4 chances of throwing each score on the come-out roll

4	8.33%
5	11.11%
6	13.88%
8	13.88%
9	11.11%
10	8.33%

table 9.5 chances of making a point once it has been made

House advantage

House advantage for bets on the pass line is 1.41 per cent. For the don't pass line the advantage varies depending on how many numbers are barred. Where no numbers are barred the house advantage is 1.402 per cent but can be as high as 4.38 per cent if three numbers are barred. To give yourself the best advantage, you should try to play on tables where no numbers are barred or, at worst, only one.

How online dice varies from traditional games

With a traditional game of dice, the shooter can have an influence on the number thrown by setting the dice in certain positions. With online dice, a random number generator selects the winning score. It is therefore virtually impossible to predict the next throw. For this reason, online dice should be played for amusement purposes only.

10 slot machines

In this chapter you will learn:
- the history of slot machines
- about types of slot machine
- about flat tops
- about progressives
- about video poker
- playing strategies
- about video poker machines.

What is a slot machine?

There are a huge variety of internet slot machines (slots for short). Most games are based on traditional mechanical machines that incorporate spinning drums around which are arranged symbols – often bells, melons, cherries, oranges and lemons. The object of the game is to line up symbols that correspond to a payout chart. There is a hierarchy of symbols. Other games resemble table games like poker, jackpot and roulette.

The history of slot machines

In 1899 Charles Fey invented the Liberty Bell, the first slot machine. To circumvent laws banning slot machines, they started selling chewing gum so they could be classified as vending machines. The chewing gum was fruit flavoured, which resulted in fruit symbols being used and in the use of the term 'fruit machine'. The bell symbol comes from the original Liberty Bell machine.

Slot machines spread across the USA. In the 1950s federal legislation was introduced that restricted their use. Las Vegas introduced slot machines as an amusement for the wives and girlfriends of high rollers. By the 1980s slot machines were as popular as table games and by the 1990s had become even more popular.

Types of slot machine

Slot machines can be divided up into flat tops, progressives and video poker machines. Flat top slots have set payouts. There will be a table of payouts for various combinations of symbol. Progressives have jackpot payouts that increase as more money is bet. Several games may be linked together to give a giant jackpot that can be equivalent to a lottery win.

What is video poker?

Video poker is a game based on five-card draw. The software deals and displays the cards. The player bets against the casino, which acts as the dealer and the banker. The object of the game is to make the highest ranking poker hand possible. Video poker differs from most other slot machines because the skill of the player affects the outcome of the game.

A winning hand is paid a fixed return. The payouts for winning hands are displayed on the casino's website. The higher the ranking of the hand, the greater the returns. The payouts vary depending on the casinos rules.

Video poker differs from a traditional game of five-card draw in a number of ways:

- There is only one player so it is not necessary to beat other players' hands.
- It is a much faster game.
- The payout odds for particular hands are fixed.
- It does not involve bluffing.

The history of video poker

Poker has been played on gaming machines since the 1800s. In 1891 Sittman and Pitt of Brooklyn began manufacturing poker card machines. They proved extremely popular and were installed in virtually all Brooklyn's licensed liquor establishments, which at that time numbered over 3000. By 1901 the machines had been redesigned so that draw poker could be played.

In the mid-1970s video poker was invented. By 1976 the first black and white video poker machines appeared. They were superseded eight months later with a colour version. Nowadays, video poker is one of the most popular casino games.

Types of video poker

There are a number of different games with slight variations in the rules. The most popular games are jacks or better, deuces wild and joker wild. Games can also be played where three hands at a time are played. For beginners, jacks or better is a simpler game to play. The returns for a royal flush on some machines are fixed, on others there is a progressive jackpot, which accumulates each time a game is played.

How to play

The aim is to make the highest ranking poker hand possible in the payout schedule. The minimum hand needed to win varies with different games.

The player makes a bet. The software will automatically deal a five-card hand.

A standard deck of 52 cards is randomly shuffled and dealt as in a normal game of poker. The player receives a five-card hand. The player then has the opportunity to improve the hand by discarding cards and being dealt new ones.

The player decides which cards to keep by clicking on the corresponding hold button. A hold can be cancelled by clicking the button a second time. The player may keep all the cards or discard any number of cards. It is possible to be dealt a winning hand with the initial five cards. When the player has decided which cards to keep, the draw/deal button is clicked. New cards will be dealt to the hand. If a hand wins it will be paid out according to the payout schedule.

Ranking of hands

Hands are ranked in the same way as five-card draw (see page 31). For games where there are wildcards, there are additional hands that include the wildcard, such as five of a kind. A royal flush made with a wildcard is considered a lower ranking hand than a regular royal flush.

Wildcards

A wildcard is a nominated card that can be used in the place of any other card. For example, the twos may be declared 'wild'. If you needed an ace to make up a hand, you could use a 2 instead of an ace. Alternatively, a joker may be wild. If, for example, you needed a queen to make up a hand, you could use the joker in its place. By allowing cards to be wild, higher ranking hands are easier to achieve. If the twos are wild then Jh, Jd, 2h, 7c, 3s would be a hand of three of a kind with jacks, where the two becomes a jack. If the joker is wild then a hand of 10h, 10d, 10c, Ah, joker would be a four of a kind. The joker becomes a 10.

With wildcards, an additional hand of five of a kind is also possible. The ranking of five of a kind depends on the game played.

Payout odds for different games

The following odds are intended only as a guide and will vary depending on where the game is played.

Jacks or better

Jacks or better is the most popular game. To win you need to get a pair of jacks or better. The minimum stake is five coins.

Payout schedule	
Hand	*Payout per coin*
Royal flush	250–800 or progressive jackpot
Straight flush	50
Four of a kind	25
Full house	6–9
Flush	5–6
Straight	4
Three of a kind	3
Two pair	2
Pair of jacks or better	1

Deuces wild

With deuces wild games, all twos are wildcards. This means that when you get a two you can use it to represent any card. If, for example, you have three aces and a two, the hand held will be four aces. Because there is a greater chance of getting a ranking hand, only hands of three of a kind or better win.

Payout schedule	
Hand	*Payout per coin*
Royal flush	varies
Four deuces	200
Royal flush with deuces	25
Five of a kind	15
Straight flush	9
Four of a kind	5
Full house	3
Flush	2
Straight	2
Three of a kind	1

Joker wild

In the game of joker wild, an additional card of a joker is added to the deck making 53 cards. The joker is a wildcard. The additional joker makes it easier to achieve higher ranking hands, which is reflected in lower payout odds than jacks or better. You also need to get a higher hand to win. You need at least two pair or better to win.

Payout schedule

Hand	Payout per coin
Royal flush	varies
Five of a kind	100
Royal flush with joker	50
Straight flush	50
Four of a kind	20
Full house	8
Flush	7
Straight	5
Three of a kind	2
Two pair	1

Playing tips

Compare the payout schedules and select the best. Progressive games offer the best value because they give you the opportunity to win a larger jackpot than flat top games.

The overall return for a game is usually expressed as a percentage. With some games it is possible to get a return of over 100 per cent if they are played over a long term. Look for a game that has already accumulated a large jackpot. In order to win the jackpot around 45 hours of fast play is required. This requires a bankroll of several thousand coins. If a large jackpot has already accumulated it will be possible to win it in a shorter time.

Always play the maximum possible stake as a smaller bet pays out lower odds. The maximum possible bet it usually five coins. A jackpot with five coins inserted pays on average 4000 coins. With only one coin inserted it pays around 250.

Learn the playing strategy for video poker. This differs from traditional five-card draw because with video poker there is no bluffing involved. Strategies like keeping a kicker to a pair are not correct for video poker.

Master jacks or better before graduating to other games. Jacks or better is the simplest game to learn.

Make sure the strategy you use is the correct one for the game you are playing. Games with wildcards like deuces and joker wild are more complex and require a different strategy to jacks or better.

Play slowly and carefully while you are learning. Hands like straights are not always immediately obvious, as the cards will rarely be displayed in the correct ascending or descending order. Don't forget that in a straight an ace can be used as a high or a low card.

Basic strategy for jacks or better

Here is a simple strategy for jacks or better that is suitable for beginners:

1 Hold any hand of a straight or over in the ranking.
2 If four cards to a royal flush are held draw one (including to a winning flush).
3 Four cards to a straight flush or a flush – draw one.
4 Three of a kind – draw two.
5 Two pair – draw one.
6 Pair – draw three.
7 Three card royal flush – draw two.
8 Four card straight – draw one.
9 Three card straight flush – draw two.
10 Two high cards J, Q, K, A – draw three.
11 Three high cards (jack and over) – hold two of the same suit. If different suits, hold the two lowest high cards.
12 Four card straight – draw one.
13 High card – draw four.
14 Nothing – draw five.

Deuces wild strategy

The strategy depends on how many deuces are held:

Four deuces – draw no cards.

Three deuces – if no royal flush or five of a kind – draw two.

Two deuces: with four of a kind or better do not draw; with four cards to a royal flush – draw one; other hands – hold the deuces and draw three.

No deuces: hold any royal flush, straight or flush.

Four cards to a royal straight, straight or flush – draw one.

Four of a kind – draw one.

Three of a kind – draw two.

One pair – draw three.

Three cards to a straight flush – draw two.

Same suited high cards 10, J, Q, K – hold two.

Nothing – draw five.

Kings or better joker wild strategy

The strategy depends on whether or not you hold a joker.

Joker held

Hold hands that are three of a kind or higher.

Hold four cards to a royal flush.

Hold any four-card straight flush and a four-card flush if it includes K or A or both.

Hold three cards to a royal flush.

Hold a paying pair of high cards (king, ace).

Hold any three cards to a straight flush.

Hold any four-card flush without king or ace.

Hold consecutive four-card straights.

If none of these, hold the joker.

No joker held

Hold all paying hands.

Hold a four-card royal flush.

Hold any four cards to a straight flush and any three cards to a royal flush.

Hold four cards to any flush.

Hold any pair of twos to queens.

Hold any three cards to a straight flush.

Hold any four-card consecutive straight.
Hold two cards to a royal flush if one of the cards is a ace or king.
Hold unsuited king and ace.
Hold king or ace alone.
Hold two suited royal flush cards lower than king or ace.
If none of these, draw five.

other games

In this chapter you will learn:
- about three-card poker/ progressive poker
- about four-card poker
- about let it ride
- about casino stud poker / Caribbean stud poker
- about pai gow poker
- about red dog
- about big six wheel/ money wheel
- about punto banco
- about sic bo
- about lotteries
- about keno.

With the exception of lotteries, these games can all be played in online casinos. The principles for playing casino games are described on page 6.

Three-card poker/progressive poker

Three card poker is a banking game. The house advantage is less than 3.5 per cent. There is no strategy involved with three-card poker, the player simply decides how much to bet. Three-card poker consists of two games that are played either separately or together – three-card ante/play and pair plus. It is played with a standard pack of 52 cards. With the pair plus game the aim is to make a ranking poker hand that is paid out at fixed odds.

With the ante-bet the aim is to make a three-card poker hand that beats the dealer's hand. The dealer needs to have at least a queen high to qualify.

The dealer and player are both dealt three cards. Pair plus bets are paid out according to the payout odds.

Ante and play

Players can also place an ante-bet against the dealer. After the cards are dealt, they can place a play bet equal to the initial ante-bet.

As only three cards are used, the rankings are not the same as traditional poker. A straight ranks higher than a flush. Aces rank both high and low. There is also no mini-royal flush.

Rankings of hands

1 Straight flush
2 Three of a kind
3 Straight
4 Flush
5 Pair
6 High card

Pair plus		Ante-bonus	
Pair	1/1	Straight	1/1
Flush	4/1	Three of a kind	4/1
Straight	6/1	Straight flush	5/1
Three of a kind	30/1		
Straight flush	40/1		

table 11.1 payout odds for three-card poker

Four-card poker

This game is similar to three-card poker. The player makes an initial bet called the 'ante-wager'. Players are dealt five cards and have to make their best four-card poker hand. The dealer is dealt six cards – five face down and one face up. He uses the six cards to make his best four-card poker hand. There are also variants where the player gets six cards and the dealer gets seven.

After looking at his cards the player can then make an additional bet up to three times the initial bet this is called the 'play wager'. Alternatively, he can fold and will lose his ante wager. The players hand must equal or beat the dealer's to win. If the player wins both bets are paid at odds of even money. For high-ranking hands, the ante-wager is paid at the odds shown in Table 11.2. There is also an additional bet called 'aces up wager' that the player can make if his hand is a pair of aces or higher.

The ranking of the hands is different from that of traditional poker.

Ranking of hands

1 Royal flush
2 Four of a kind
3 Straight flush
4 Three of a kind
5 Straight
6 Two pair
7 Flush
8 One pair
9 High card

Ante-wager	Bonus	Aces up
Four of a kind	25/1	
Straight flush	20/1	
Three of a kind	2/1	9/1
Flush		6/1
Straight		4/1
Two pair		2/1
Pair of aces		1/1

table 11.2 odds for four-card poker

Let it ride

Let it ride poker is a banking game. The aim is to get a pair of tens or better using three cards dealt to the player and two community cards dealt to the dealer.

The player makes three equal bets. The dealer then gives each player three cards and the dealer is dealt two community cards, face down. After seeing their first three cards the player may take back one of their three bets or let it ride. One of the community cards is then revealed. The player then has the option to take out another bet or let it ride. The second community card is revealed. If the player fails to get at least a pair of tens all bets are lost. If a hand containing at least a pair of tens is held, bets are then paid out according to Table 11.3.

Tens or over	1/1
Two pair	2/1
Three of a kind	3/1
Straight	5/1
Flush	8/1
Full house	11/1
Four of a kind	50/1
Straight flush	200/1
Royal flush	1000/1
House advantage	3.5%

table 11.3 odds for let it ride

Let it ride strategy

Let the first bet ride if your first three cards are:

a pair of tens or better

any three cards to a royal flush

three-card straight flush or inside straight flush.

three-card double inside straight flush with two high cards
  (10 or higher)

10, J, Q.

Let the second bet ride if your first four cards are:

pair of tens or better

any four cards of the same suit

four-card straight (open end)

four high cards (10 or higher).

Casino stud poker/Caribbean stud poker

The history of Caribbean stud poker

Caribbean stud poker was invented in the mid-1980s on the Caribbean island of Aruba. It began to be played on cruise ships and gradually spread to casinos around the world. It differs from other poker games as it is played against the casino, which acts as banker. Instead of playing for a pot, the winning hands are paid out at fixed odds. There is also no bluffing involved. In order to win, you have only to beat the dealer's hand. The other players' hands do not affect the outcome of your bets.

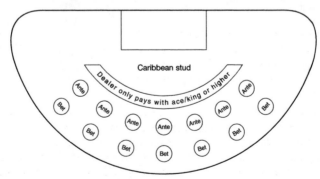

figure 11.1 Caribbean stud poker layout

The game

The object of the game is to win by having a five-card poker hand that ranks higher than the dealer's. Each player makes an ante-bet and is dealt five cards face down. The dealer receives four cards face down and one card face up.

Players then look at their cards and have the option to play or fold. If a player folds, his ante-bet is lost. If a player decides to continue, he must then make a further bet of double his ante-bet.

The dealer's hand is then revealed. He must have an ace and a king or higher in order to play his hand. If a player's hand beats the dealer's, the ante-bet is paid at evens. See Table 11.4 for the odds for the second bet. If the dealer does not have at least an ace and a king then a player is paid even money on the ante-bet and the additional bet is void (not lost). If, however, the dealer's hand beats the player's, both bets are lost.

One pair or less	1/1 (even)
Two pair	2/1
Three of a kind	3/1
Straight	4/1
Flush	5/1
Full house	7/1
Four of a kind	20/1
Straight flush	50/1
Royal flush	100/1

table 11.4 payout odds for an additional bet in Caribbean stud poker

If the dealer and the player play the same poker hand, the remaining cards are taken into consideration. If all five cards are equal, the hand is void (the bet is not lost). Neither the ante-bet nor the additional bet is paid. The type of suit makes no difference to the hand.

The disadvantage of this game is that you are relying purely on luck. There is no skill involved. You do not have the opportunity to bluff. In poker games where you are playing for a pot, you are still able to win even with a poor hand but with Caribbean stud poker, if you have a poor hand, you stand little chance of winning.

The minimum odds in this game are evens. In a normal game of poker with, for example, seven players, you would have odds of at least 6/1 and quite often a great deal better. The odds paid for the additional bet are also poor compared to the chances of achieving them. Odds of 100/1 are paid for a royal flush, yet your chances of being dealt one are 649,739/1. The only advantage you have is that you know how much each game is going to cost you.

Caribbean stud poker should be played only for amusement purposes. If you want to win money, you are better advised to play games where you are contesting for a pot.

Caribbean stud strategy

Caribbean stud poker has a house advantage of 5.26 per cent. By playing the following strategy it is possible to cut the house advantage to about 2.6 per cent. You need to decide whether to play or fold your hand. You should fold if you don't get a minimum hand of an ace and a king.

Players should raise when they hold any pair or an ace and a king. With some hands you need to match the dealer's up card to reduce the possibility that the dealer has a pair.

Player's hand	Dealer's hand	Action
Lower than A K		Fold
Any pair	Any up card	Raise
A K Q J x	Any up card	Raise
A K Q xx	Must match one card	Raise
A K J xx	Must match one card	Raise
A K 10 xx	Must match one card	Raise
The $1 progressive jackpot bet is extremely difficult to win. It is not worthwhile playing until the level of the jackpot exceeds $263,000.		

table 11.5 details of hands that should be raised

Pai gow poker

In pai gow poker, each player in turn has the option of being banker. The game is a mixture of the Chinese game pai gow and American poker. It is played with one deck of 52 cards, plus one joker. The joker can be used only as an ace or to complete a straight, a flush, a straight flush or a royal flush.

The player is dealt seven cards. The cards are arranged to make two hands: a two-card hand and a five-card hand. The five-card hand must rank higher or be equal to the two-card hand (see Table 11.6).

The object of the game is for both of your hands to rank higher than both of your opponent's hand. Your two-card hand must rank higher than your opponent's two card hand and your five card hand must rank higher than you opponent's five card hand.

Five-card hand	Two-card hand
Five aces (five aces plus the joker)	One pair
Royal flush	High card
Straight flush	
Four of a kind	
Full house	
Flush	
Straight	
Three of a kind	
Two pair	
One pair	
High card	

table 11.6 ranking of hands in pai gow poker

If one of your hands ranks the same as your opponent's hand, this is a tie (or copy hand). The banker wins all ties. If you win one hand but lose the other, this is known as a 'push'. In push, no money is exchanged. Winning hands are paid even money, less a 5 per cent commission. Losing hands lose the money bet.

The game

The dealer and each player in turn are all given the opportunity to be banker. You can only be banker if you bet against the dealer the last time he was banker. You need to have sufficient chips to pay the bets should your opponent win.

You arrange your cards into the two hands. The dealer will then make his hands. Each hand is compared to the dealer's hands. If the player wins one hand and loses the other, the bet is void. If you wrongly set your hand, you lose.

The major disadvantage to this game is that you are relying on the luck of the deal – there is no skill involved. If your cards are poor, there is no opportunity to bluff. The dealer plays his hand if he has the minimum required and does not drop out of the betting.

As with Caribbean stud poker, the odds are also poor compared to playing for a pot.

See Figure 11.2. Player A has beaten the dealer's five-card hand but has failed to beat the two-card hand. This is a push – the money bet is not lost.

dealer's hands

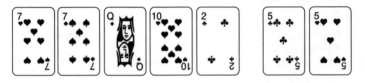

players' hands

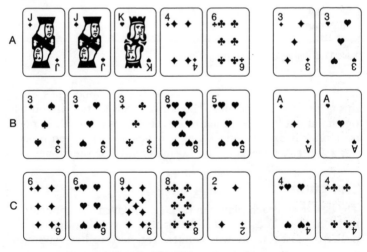

figure 11.2 example hands in pai gow poker

Player B has beaten both hands. His bet is paid at even money less 5 per cent commission.

Player C has failed to beat the dealer's five and two-card hand. He loses his bet.

Pai gow poker strategy

The strategy for pai gow poker is based on how you set the hands. The five-card hand needs to be higher than the two-card hand. There will be situations where, for example, you have two pair. Depending on the cards it is sometimes advantageous to split up the two pair and put the high pair in the back hand and the low pair in the front hand. The strategy for setting the hands with the various different combinations of card is shown below.

Strategy

Five-card hand = back
Two-card hand = front

No pair:
Back – highest card
Front – second and third highest cards

One pair:
Back – pair
Front – highest other two cards

Two pair:
AA, KK, QQ, JJ
Back – high pair
Front – small pair

77 to 10,10 with an ace:
Back – two pair
Front – ace

22 to 66 with a king:
Back – two pair
Front – king

22 to 66 with no king:
Back – high pair
Front – low pair

Three pair:
Back – low pairs
Front – high pair

Three of a kind:
- With aces:
  Back – pair of aces
  Front – ace and next highest card

- Two sets of three of a kind:
  Back – the lower three of a kind
  Front – pair from the higher set

Straight, flush, straight flush:
- With no pair:
  Back – complete hand
  Front – two highest other cards

- With one pair:
  Back – complete hand
  Front – two highest other cards

- With two pair:
  Use two-pair strategy

- With three of a kind:
  Back – complete hand
  Front – pair

Full house:
Front – pair

Four of a kind:
- Jacks to aces – split
- 7 to 10 with an ace:
  Back – four of a kind
  Front – Ace
- 7 to 10 no ace – split
- 6 or below – do not split
- With three of a kind:
  Back – full house
  Front – highest pair

Five aces:
Back – three aces
Front – pair of aces

Example

With K, J, 3, K, 9, 7, J there is a possible hand of two pair. This would be set as follows:

Back – K, K, 9, 7, 3

Front – J, J

Red dog

Red dog is a simple card game. The object of the game is simply that players bet that the value of a third card dealt will be between the value of the first two cards dealt.

> **Card values**
>
> Cards 2 to 10 have their face value
>
> Jacks count as 11
>
> Queens count as 12
>
> Kings count as 13
>
> Aces count as 14

Playing the game

Two cards are dealt face up. A third card is drawn and placed face up between the first two cards. Players win when the value of the third card drawn is in between the values of the first and second card.

Betting

Bets are placed in the box marked 'bet'. After the first two cards have been dealt, players have the option of making an additional bet up to the value of their original bet. These bets are placed in the box marked 'raise'. This additional bet must be placed before a third card is dealt.

Odds paid

The spread between the first two cards dealt determines the odds paid. The spread is the number of card values between the first two cards drawn.

If the first two cards dealt were a 6 and an 8, the spread would be one, because one card comes between them. If the first two cards dealt were an ace and a 2, the spread would be 11.

Consecutive pair

If the first two cards dealt are of consecutive value, for example, 4 and 5, Q and K, 2 and 3, there is no spread. They are called a consecutive pair. It is not possible to raise this bet.

Pair

If the first two cards dealt are a pair, for example, two sixes or two queens, the bet is void (a tie). This bet cannot be raised.

Three of a kind

This is where the first two cards are a pair and the third card drawn is of equal value.

Odds paid on red dog

One-card spread 5/1

Two-card spread 4/1

Three-card spread 2/1

Four- or more card spread 1/1 (evens)

Red dog should be considered for amusement purposes only. The odds paid are poor compared with your chances of making the point. There is no way that you can influence the outcome and you are dependent entirely on the luck of the draw.

Big six wheel/money wheel

Big six wheel is a game played on a vertical spinning wheel. The wheel is divided into sections marked with symbols and payout amounts. Players bet on where the wheel will stop. The betting layout is marked with boxes that correspond to the sections of the wheel. To place a bet you simply put your chips in the corresponding box. In Australia, a similar game is played called big money wheel.

American wheel

$1	Evens	11.11%
$2	2/1	16.67%
$5	5/1	22.22%
$10	10/1	18.52%
$20	20/1	22.22%
Joker/logo	40/1	24.07%
	45/1	14.81%

Australian wheel		
$1	Evens	7.69%
$3	3/1	7.69%
$5	5/1	7.69%
$10	11/1	7.69%
$23	23/1	7.69%
Joker/logo	47/1	7.69%

table 11.7 payout odds and house advantage

Punto banco

Punto banco is a popular card game based on baccara. The games of chemin de fer, baccarat and punto banco are all similar games with the same basic principles with different rules on where they are played. All winning bets are paid by the casino but players take turns to control the bank. Generally, four decks of cards are used.

The history of punto banco

Baccara (meaning zero) has its origins in medieval Italy. It soon spread to France where it became chemin de fer (railway, due to the shoe passing around the table on 'tracks'). Baccara proved to be popular among the aristocracy. Later a slightly different version arrived in England that was called punto banco. The game spread to Latin America and, as a direct result of the closing of Cuban casinos in the 1950s, the game was introduced to Las Vegas where it was known as shimmy. Today the game is played in various forms in casinos around the world.

The game

Using a maximum of three cards, the players try to make a score as close as possible to 9.

Tens and court cards (kings, queens, jacks) have a value of 0.

Aces count as 1.

Cards 2 to 9 have their face value.

Scoring

The values of the cards are added to give the score. Cards with a joint value of 10 are given a value of 0.

Example

7 + 3 = 10 score = 0
8 + 2 = 10 score = 0
6 + 4 = 10 score = 0
J + K = 0 score = 0
K + A = 1 score = 1

Where the cards total more than 10, only the last figure of the total is counted as the score.

Example

8 + 6 = 14 score = 4
10 + 9 = 19 score = 9, known as a 'natural'

The deal

The cards are shuffled. Each player makes a bet. The players and the banker each receive two cards. The dealer announces the totals of each hand. If the totals are 8 or 9 that is a 'natural' and no further cards are dealt.

There are set rules that determine whether or not a third card should be dealt.

Player having		
1 2 3 4 5 0	draws a card	
6 7	stands	
8 9	natural, banker cannot draw	
Banker having	draws when giving	stands when player's third card is
3	1 2 3 4 5 6 7 8 9 0	8
4	2 3 4 5 6 7	1 8 9 0
5	4 5 6 7	1 2 3 8 9 0
6	6 7	1 2 3 4 5 8 9 0
7	stands	
8 9	natural, player cannot draw	

---

table 11.8 chart detailing when an extra card is drawn on punto banco

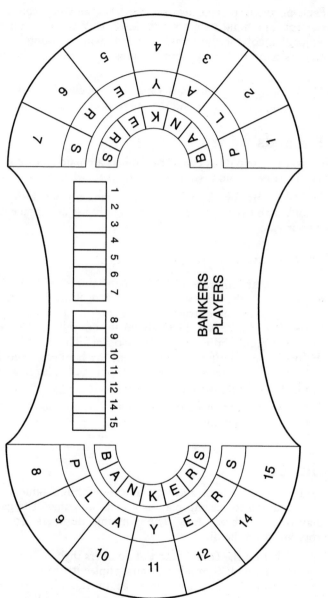

figure 11.3 betting layout for punto banco

Betting

Each player is playing against the bank and not against one another. The hand with a score closest to 9 wins. The bets are either 'banco' for the bank's hand to win or 'punto' for the player's hand to win. In some casinos, it is also possible to bet on a tie.

The layout of the tables varies but they are clearly marked with boxes where the banco and the punto bets should be placed.

The odds

Punto bets are paid at evens. Banco bets are paid at 19/20 (evens less 5 per cent commission).

The odds paid for a tie vary but are commonly 8/1. However, it is not worth betting on a tie as the high house advantage makes it poor value.

How to play

Two cards are alternately dealt to the punto and the banco hands. Where the first two cards total 8 or 9 this is known as a 'natural' and wins outright without the need to take further cards. When there is a tie, the hand is replayed. A total of 0 is the worst hand and is known as 'baccara'. The person holding the bank will continue to do so until the banker's hand loses. The bank is then passed to the right, but if the player wishes it can be passed earlier.

The players do not need to make any decisions, so they cannot influence the outcome.

Sic bo

Sic bo is based on an ancient Chinese gambling game and has been adapted for casino play as a banking game. The game is played with three dice. The winning numbers are those uppermost on the dice.

Players bet on the combination of numbers thrown. Bets can be made on individual numbers, pairs, triples (three of a kind) or combinations of any two or three of the dice. The house advantage varies between 2.78 and 33.33 per cent depending on which bets are made and where the game is played.

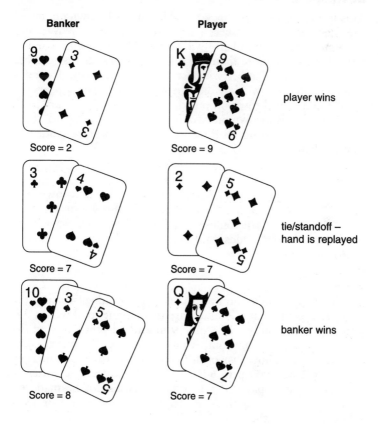

figure 11.4 example hands in punto banco

The dealer will announce 'place your bets'. Players place their bets on the layout on the box marked with the desired outcome. For example, if you want to bet on big, you simply place your chip in the box marked big. The dealer will announce 'no more bets'. The dice are shaken. The dealer announces the winning numbers and the winning bets are paid out.

Types of bet

There are 50 bets that can be played. The bets can be divided into seven different types.

Individual number

This is a bet on one particular number being thrown on any of the three dice. The numbers 1 to 6 inclusive can be played. For example, a bet on number 4 will win if a 4 is thrown on any of the three dice. If more than one 4 is thrown, the bet is paid out at greater odds. The bet will lose if no 4 is thrown. The odds paid depend on how many dice the selected number appears on. If the number is thrown on one die, odds of evens 1/1 are paid. If the number is thrown on two dice odds of 2/1 are paid. If the number is thrown on all three dice odds of 3/1 are paid. The house advantage is 7.87 per cent.

Double

A double is a bet on two particular numbers being thrown. For example, a bet on 3 and 5 will win if 3 is thrown on one dice and 5 on another. All combinations of numbers are marked on the betting layout. Odds paid are 5/1. The house advantage is 16.67 per cent.

Totals

The winning numbers on all three dice are added to find the total. For example if 6, 4 and 2 are thrown the total will be 12. Bets made on number 12 would win and all other bets on the totals would lose. Any total from 4 to 17 can be played. The odds depend on how easy or difficult it is to throw a total. They start at 6/1 and go up to 60/1. The house advantage varies as different casinos pay different odds. Bets cannot be made on scores of 3 and 18 as these are triples. If a score of 3 or 18 is made all bets on the totals lose.

Total	Odds	House advantage	Odds	House advantage	Odds	House advantage
4 or 17	60/1	29.1%	50/1	12.5%		
5 or 16	18/1	47.2%	30/1	13.89%		
6 or 15	14/1	30.56%	17/1	16.67%	18/1	12.04%
7 or 14	12/1	9.72%				
8 or 13	8/1	12.5%				
9 or 12	6/1	18.98%				
10 or 11	6/1	12.5%				

table 11.9 payout odds and house advantage for each score

Small or big

Small is a bet on a score of between 4 and 10. For example if the 3, 4 and 2 are thrown the total is 9, which would be a winning bet. Big is a bet on a score of between 11 and 17. For example, if 6, 5 and 3 are thrown the total is 14, which would be a winning number. Bets on small or big lose if a triple (three of a kind) is thrown. The house advantage is 2.78 per cent.

Triple of a particular number

A triple is the same score on each dice. For example, three fives or three fours. A particular triple is a triple made with one particular number. For example, if a triple of three fours is played, the bet will lose if three fives are thrown. The odds paid on winning bets varies. At odds of 150/1, the house advantage is 30.09 per cent. At odds of 180/1, the house advantage is 16.2 per cent.

Any triple

Any triple is a bet on any three of a kind. For odds of 24/1, the house advantage is 30.56 per cent. For odds of 30/1, the house advantage is 13.89 per cent.

Any pair

Any pair is a bet that two of the dice will have the same score. For example, a throw of 3, 3, 5 would win. For odds of 8/1, the house advantage is 33.33 per cent. For odds of 10/1, the house advantage is 18.52 per cent.

Betting layout

The betting layout is divided into four rows. The bottom row is marked with the single-number bets. The next row is marked with the two-number bets. The following row has the bets on the total of the three dice. The top row has the big and small, triple and double bets. The payout odds for each bet are marked on the layout.

Strategy

There is no strategy to predict the winning numbers; players simply rely on luck. The best bet to make is the big or small bet as this has the lowest house advantage. The worst bet to make is any pair that has the highest house advantage.

Lotteries

A lottery is a game in which players try to predict what numbers will be drawn from a pool of numbers. For example, in the UK National Lottery, players select six numbers between 1 and 49 inclusive. The UK lottery is run by Camelot. The draw takes place on Saturdays and Wednesdays. The numbers 1 to 49 inclusive are printed on balls. These balls are dropped into a machine that mixes them and randomly selects seven balls – six balls and a bonus ball. A player who correctly predicts the first six balls selected wins the jackpot. If there is more than one winner, the prize is shared between them. There are other prizes for predicting three, four and five numbers. If there is no winner, the jackpot is rolled over to the next week. It is possible to bet on the UK National Lottery online. In addition to the main lottery, a variety of games is offered. The odds against winning the jackpot are huge – 1,398,3815/1. Lotteries are games of chance where you are reliant on luck rather than skill to win. The amount won varies depending on how many people participate. It can be millions of pounds. The money bet is distributed as follows:

winners, 50%
good causes, 28%
government (lottery duty), 12%
sales commission to retailers, 5%
operating costs, 4.5%
profit to Camelot, 0.5%.

To play the UK National Lottery online you must be aged 16 or over, resident in the UK or Isle of Man and have a valid debit card linked to a UK or Isle of Man bank. You will need to register with the site and give personal details. You may be required to prove your age and identity.

EuroMillions can also be played via the National Lottery site (see page 196). It is a lottery that combines the pools from nine European countries – Austria, Belgium, England, France, Ireland, Luxembourg, Portugal, Spain and Switzerland. Winnings can be as high as €50 million.

There are websites selling tickets for lotteries around the world. However, you should be cautious about buying such tickets. Before playing you should read the terms and conditions, as there are often residency requirements. Many lotteries only allow tickets to be sold within particular areas. For example, in the USA, state and federal laws prohibit the sale of lottery tickets via the internet. Tickets for the Florida Lottery can only be sold inside the state of Florida.

Keno

The history of keno

Keno is based on a lottery that has its origins in China. Over 2000 years ago, Cheung Heung came up with the idea of organizing a lottery to raise funds for his province's army. It proved to be a huge success and even funded the building of the Great Wall of China. The game was brought to America in the 1800s when thousands of Chinese immigrants worked in mines and on the building of the railroad. It was adapted for casino play and was originally known as the Chinese lottery. Later, the name was changed to keno. It is now played in casinos around the world.

Keno is a lottery that is popular in American casinos. Thousands of games are played each day. Players choose between one and 20 numbers. The payouts for different combinations of numbers are also displayed. Players need to simply check the ticket for the game played along with the result to find out if they have a winner.

Keno is played for small stakes and potentially huge jackpots.

If you win $1500 or more in American casinos, you will need to fill in a tax form (W2 G). Losses can be offset against winnings but is necessary to keep old receipts as proof.

glossary

abandoned racing has been called off at that particular meeting

accumulator a bet on any number of selections, in different races, where the winnings on the first horse go onto the second and then onto the third and then onto the fourth and so on

all in in poker, a player who runs out of funds may still play for the portion of the pot he has contributed to

allowance the weight conceded by professional jockeys to apprentices or conditionals to compensate for their inexperience

also-ran a horse that lost

anchor box the player who is dealt cards first is sitting on the anchor box

ante initial bet

apprentice a young jockey tied by contract to a trainer while learning flat racing

arbitrage back and lay or buy and sell in the same market to make a profit

AWT all-weather fibre-sand track

back bet that a horse will win

back all bet that all the horses in a race will win

banker a horse that is strongly fancied and is often the main selection in multiple bets

basic strategy a playing strategy that reduces the house advantage in blackjack

blackjack a score of 21 made with an ace and any other card worth 10

blind bet bet made before a hand is seen

bluff pretend you have a good hand in poker

board community cards in hold 'em and Omaha

board price the current price on offer for a horse

bookies betting shop or bookmaker's

book percentage a figure that shows the profit of a book. The book percentage minus 100 gives the percentage profit or loss that is made by betting on all runners. A figure greater than 100 is its profit. The percentage less than 100 is the percentage loss on a book

boxed in when a horse cannot overtake another because one or more horses block its path

break a score over 21 in blackjack

brought down a horse that has fallen due to the actions of another horse

bumper a flat race for horses bred for national hunt

burlington bertie a price of 100/30

burnt cards cards that are discarded without being seen by the players

button marker used to denote the dealer in poker

call bet the same as the previous player in poker

carpet a price of 3/1

carré bet on four numbers on roulette

cheval bet on two numbers on roulette

clerk of the course race course official who manages the race day

clerk of the scales Jockey Club official who ensures horses carry the correct weight.

closing a bet (spread betting) placing a second bet of the same size in the opposite direction of the initial bet

co-favourites where there is more than one favourite

colours silk shirts worn by the jockeys

colt young male horse, aged 4 years and under

come-out first roll of the dice

commission the amount charged for the services supplied by a betting exchange or spread betting firm

community cards cards laid face up in games like hold 'em and Omaha that may be used by all players to make a hand

conditional young jockey tied by contract to a trainer while learning national hunt racing

conditions race a race where horses carry weight according to factors such as age, sex, whether they have won before or the type of race won

connections people related to a horse, such as the trainer and owner

craps dice; a score of two, three or 12 in dice

court cards king, queen and jack

dead heat where a race is a tie for either the winner or one of the placed horses

dead man's hand two pair of aces over eights in poker

decimal odds odds where the stake is included in the price. For example 2/1 is 3.0

deuce two

dolly marker used on roulette to show the winning number

double carpet a price of 33/1

down bet a bet that the result will be lower than the lower end of the quote. Also called a sell

draw the position of a horse in the starting stalls

drift odds that lengthen

dutching betting different stakes on several horse in a race to give the same payout no matter which of the selections wins

dwelt slow at the start

edge the profit a casino makes on bets usually expressed as a percentage

en plein bet on one number on roulette (straight up)

evens a price of 1/1

favourite the horse with the lowest price

FC an abbreviation for forecast

field the runners in a race

filly a female horse up to 4 years old

first base the player who is dealt cards first is sitting at first base

first time out a horse running in its first race

flat tops slot machines with fixed payouts

flop first three community cards dealt on hold 'em or Omaha

fold surrender from the game

form a record of a horse's previous racing performance

furlong an eighth of a mile (201 metres)

gelding a castrated male horse

gentleman jockey an amateur jockey

going the condition of the racing surface

going down the horses are on their way to the start

grand £1000

green a description of an inexperienced horse

hand a measure of a horse's height, equivalent to four inches

hardways same score on both dice

hedge place additional bets to guarantee a profit

hit take another card

hole card dealer's down card

hole cards cards in the player's hand

home stretch the length of straight track before the finishing post

hopping one-roll betting

house advantage the profit a casino makes on bets, usually expressed as a percentage

IBAS the Independent Betting Arbitration Service, a British organization that settles disputes with bookmakers on the punters' behalf when the bookmaker is a member of the scheme

impair odd

index bet a bet where the performance is measured by awarding points for a particular outcome

in-running betting on an event as it happens

inspection due either to the weather or condition of the course, a decision will be made about whether or not racing can go ahead

irons stirrups

joint favourites two horses are favourite

jolly the favourite

judge Jockey Club official who declares the race result and the distances between runners

juvenile a 2-year-old horse in flat racing, a 3- or 4-year-old-horse in jump racing

lame a horse that is having difficulty walking or is limping

lay bet that a horse will lose

lay all bet that all the horses in a race will lose

layers bookmakers

laying off bookmakers practice of reducing betting liability by betting with other bookmakers

long shot a horse with high odds

maiden a horse or rider that has not previously won a race

makeup the result on which a bet is settled

manqué low

mare female horse aged 5 years and over

match a race where there are only two horses competing

maximum makeup a maximum limit on the result

miss out losing score in dice

muck pile where the losing hands are placed

nap the top tip of the day from a racing tipster

natural a score of 7 or 11 on the first roll of dice; a score of eight or nine in punto banco

no offers no price is offered by the bookmakers. N/O is displayed on the screen

novice a jump racing term: a novice hurdler is a horse that has not won a hurdle race before the current season, a novice chaser is a horse that has not won a steeplechase before the current season

objection a complaint from a jockey that, in his opinion, the rules of racing have been broken

odds on a price lower than evens

off the race has started

open make the first bet

open bet a bet that has not been closed or settled

outsider a horse with little chance of winning

over-round the profit on a book

overbroke a book with a loss

pacer a horse in harness racing which moves its legs on one side of its body in unison

pair (roulette) even: two cards of the same value, for example two aces

pari-mutuel the prices quoted by the French tote

pass take no further cards

passé high

pattern created in 1971 to ensure that the major European races are spread out across the season and do not clash. Pattern races are classified in groups one to three with group one being the most important races and including the classics

penalty a weight added to the handicap weight of a horse

photo finish a close race where the aid of a photograph is needed to determine the result

picture cards king, queen and jack

plate a shoe worn by a horse for racing

plater a horse that runs in selling races

pocket cards cards in the players hand in games like hold 'em and Omaha

pokies video poker machines

pot money played for in poker

press increase bets

prop bets proposition bets (craps bets and hardways)

pulled up a horse that drops out of the race after the off

punter someone who bets

push a bet that is tied

racecard a programme for the day's racing

rag a horse with little chance of winning (an outsider)

raise make an increased bet

rake a charge made by the casino for the use of its facilities, usually a percentage of the pot

rating a measure of the performance of a horse on a scale of 0–140, where 140 is the highest

run a straight reduction factor. The percentage that will be deducted from odds on a betting exchange in the event of a withdrawn horse

rule 4 a deduction made from the prices due to the withdrawal of a horse from a race

scratching a horse that is withdrawn from a race

seven out a score of 7 after the come out roll in dice

shooter person who throws the dice

showdown when the players reveal their hands in poker

sidewheeler a pacer in harness racing

SP an abbreviation for starting price

spread the difference between what a spread betting firm predicts and the outcome

spread a plate lose a horse shoe

stake amount of money bet

stallion male horse that has retired from racing and is mating mares

stand take no more cards

standoff a tie

starter the person responsible for starting the race

steeplechase a race over obstacles

steward Jockey Club official who is responsible for checking that the rules of racing are followed

stewards' enquiry an inquiry into whether or not the rules of racing have been broken

straight slots slot machines with fixed payouts

stud where horses are bred

stud book a book that contains the pedigree of thoroughbred race horses

system a method of betting that is supposed to favour the player

thoroughbred a horse bred for racing that is registered in the general stud book

tipster a person who is employed by a newspaper to recommend horses that are likely to win

tissue prices early prices offered before a betting market has been formed

trip the distance of the race

trips three of a kind

trotter a horse in harness racing that moves with a diagonal gait

under orders the race is about to start

up bet or buy in spread betting, a bet that the outcome will be higher than the prediction

vigorish commission

walkover a race with only runner. In order to be declared the winner, the horse must walk over the course. Where there are obstacles, the horse need not jump over them, but may walk around

weigh-in after each race the jockeys on the winning and placed horses must weigh in to confirm that they are carrying the same weight as at the start of the race

yearling a horse from 1 January to 31 December of the year following its birth

Gamblers' help organizations

Great Britain

GamCare
2 & 3 Baden Place
Crosby Row
London SE1 1YW
Tel 020 7378 5200
Fax 020 7378 5237
Helpline 0845 6000 133 (24 hour, 7 days a week)
Email info@gamcare.org.uk
www.gamcare.org.uk/

United States

Gamblers Intergroup
PO Box 7
New York
New York 10116
Tel 212 903 4400

Australia

Gamblers Anonymous
PO Box 142
Burwood
NSW 1805
Tel (02) 9564 1574
www.gamblersanonymous.org.au/

Regulatory bodies and arbitration services

British Horseracing Board
Via their website tickets can be purchased for any racing event in Britain.
www.britishhorseracing.com/

Financial Services Authority
FSA Consumer Helpline 0845 606 1234 open 8am to 6pm
The helpline can tell you if a spread betting firm is authorized.
www.fsa.gov.uk/

Fraud Watch International
www.fraudwatchinternational.com/

Gambling Commission
www.gamblingcommission.org.uk/

Independent Betting Arbitration Service (IBAS)
PO Box 4011
London E14 5BB
Tel 0207 529 7670
www.ibas-uk.com/

Interactive Gaming Council Canada
175-2906 West Broadway
Vancouver BC V6K 2G8
Canada
Tel 604 732 3833
Fax 604 732 3866
www.igcouncil.org/contact.php

UK bookmakers

Coral
www.coral.co.uk/

Totesport
www.totesport.com/

Ladbrokes
www.ladbrokes.com/

Victor Chandler
www.vcbet.com/

Paddy Power
www.paddypower.com/

William Hill
www.willhill.com/

Tote Ireland
www.tote.ie/=

Betting exchanges

Betdaq
www.betdaq.co.uk/

GG-Bet
www.gg.com/

Betfair
www.betfair.com/

Spread betting firms

Sporting Index
www.sportingindex.com/

SportsSpread.com
www.sportsspread.com/

SpreadEx
www.spreadex.com/

Online poker rooms

Gaming Club
Licensed by the Government of Gibraltar
www.gamingclubpoker.com/

Ladbrokespoker.com
Operated by the world's biggest betting and gaming company. Licensed in Gibraltar and regulated by British gaming rules. Their card-shuffling procedure is audited
www.ladbrokespoker.com/

Paradise Poker
Located in San José, Costa Rica. Their card-shuffling procedure is audited
www.paradisepoker.com/

PartyPoker
Licenced and regulated by the Government of Gibraltar.
www.partypoker.com/

Poker Stars.com
Located in San José, Costa Rica. Their card-shuffling procedure is audited.
www.pokerstars.com/

Lotteries

UK National Lottery
www.national-lottery.co.uk/

Horse racing publications

Great Britain

In the Know
Monthly horse racing magazine.
www.itkonline.com/

Inside Edge
Monthly magazine covering all forms of gambling.
www.inside-edge-mag.co.uk/

Pacemaker
www.pacemakerworld.com/

Raceform
Publishers of horseracing information, including the official formbook and three weekly newspapers:

Racing & Football Outlook – weekly preview of forthcoming racing and football fixtures with tips and statistics.

Raceform Update – racing data, expert analysis and tips for racing.

Weekend Special – tips for weekend racing.
www.raceform.co.uk/

Racing Ahead
Monthly horse racing magazine aimed at punters.
www.racingahead.net/

Racing Post
Daily newspaper.
www.racingpost.co.uk/

Timeform
Publishers of horse racing publications including *Timeform Race Cards*, the weekly *Timeform Black Book*, *Racehorses*, *Chasers & Hurdlers*, *Timeform Perspective*, *Computer Timeform* and *Timeform Horses to Follow*.
www.timeform.com/

United States of America

American Turf Monthly
Thoroughbred handicapping magazine.
www.americanturf.com/

Daily Racing Form
www.drf.com/

The Blood-Horse
Monthly magazine.
services.bloodhorse.com/

Thoroughbred Times
Weekly magazine.
www.thoroughbredtimes.com/

Canada

The Canadian Sportsman
Biweekly harness racing publication.
www.canadiansportsman.ca/

Trot Magazine
Monthly magazine.
www.standardbredcanada.ca/

Australia and New Zealand

Australasian Turf Monthly
www.americanturf.com/

Harness Racing New Zealand
www.hrnz.co.nz/

South Africa

Sporting Post
www.sportingpost.co.za/

The Gulf

RaceWeek
www.raceweek.co.uk/

index